Hearty
Soups & Stews

Contents

Fire On High

This hot medley of spicy recipes is sure to keep you warm all winter long.

Spicy Black Bean & Sausage Stew

· ·

1 tablespoon olive oil
½ cup chopped onion
¼ cup chopped green bell pepper
4 ounces low-fat smoked sausage, cut into ¼-inch pieces
2 cloves garlic, minced
1 cup drained canned black beans, rinsed
¾ cup undrained no-salt-added stewed tomatoes
1½ teaspoons dried oregano leaves
¾ teaspoon ground cumin
2 tablespoons minced fresh parsley
Hot pepper sauce, to taste
Hot cooked rice (optional)

1. Heat oil in medium skillet over medium heat. Add onion, bell pepper and sausage. Cook and stir 3 to 4 minutes or until vegetables are tender. Add garlic; cook and stir 1 minute.

2. Stir in beans, tomatoes with juice, oregano and cumin, breaking up tomatoes into small chunks with spoon. Bring to a boil; reduce heat to low.

3. Cover and simmer 20 minutes, stirring occasionally. Stir in parsley and hot pepper sauce. Serve with hot cooked rice, if desired.   *Makes 2 servings*

Spicy Black Bean & Sausage Stew

Chicken Tortilla Soup

....

2 large ripe avocados,
     halved and pitted
4 teaspoons TABASCO®
     brand Green Pepper
     Sauce, divided
½ teaspoon salt <u>or</u> to taste
3 (14½-ounce) cans
     chicken broth
3 boneless, skinless chicken
     breast halves (about
     1 pound)
2 tablespoons uncooked
     rice
1 large tomato, seeded and
     chopped
½ cup chopped onion
¼ cup finely chopped
     cilantro
   Tortilla chips
½ cup (2 ounces) shredded
     Monterey Jack cheese

Scoop out avocado into medium bowl and mash with fork. Add 1½ teaspoons TABASCO® Green Pepper Sauce and salt; blend gently but thoroughly. Set aside.

Heat chicken broth to boiling in 4-quart saucepan. Add chicken breast halves; reduce heat and cook until chicken is opaque.

Remove chicken and cut into bite-size pieces. Add rice and cook about 15 minutes or until tender. Return chicken to saucepan. Just before serving, stir in tomato, onion, cilantro and remaining 2½ teaspoons TABASCO® Green Pepper Sauce.

To serve, break small handful of tortilla chips into bottom of each bowl. Ladle soup over tortilla chips. Top with cheese and 1 rounded tablespoon avocado mixture. Serve immediately with additional TABASCO® Green Pepper Sauce, if desired.

Makes 8 servings

Chicken Tortilla Soup

Spicy Chili with Cornmeal Dumplings

....

1½ pounds ground beef
1¼ cups finely chopped
    green bell peppers
½ cup chopped onion
1 clove garlic, minced
½ cup A.1.® Original or
    A.1.® BOLD & SPICY
    Steak Sauce
3 large tomatoes, chopped
    (about 3½ cups)
1 (1¼-ounce) package taco
    seasoning mix
¼ teaspoon ground cumin
½ teaspoon crushed red
    pepper flakes
1 (6.5-ounce) package corn
    muffin mix
⅓ cup milk
1 egg
½ cup shredded Cheddar
    cheese (2 ounces)
¼ cup sliced green onions

Cook beef, green peppers, onion and garlic in large skillet over medium-high heat until beef is browned, stirring occasionally to break up beef. Stir in steak sauce, tomatoes, seasoning mix, cumin and pepper flakes. Heat to a boil; reduce heat.

Cover; simmer 10 to 15 minutes to blend flavors.

Meanwhile, mix corn muffin mix according to package directions, using milk and egg. Drop batter into 6 mounds on chili mixture. Cover; simmer 10 to 12 minutes. (Do not lift cover.) Sprinkle with cheese and green onions. Serve immediately.

Makes 6 servings

Pecos "Red" Stew

....

**2 pounds boneless pork
   shoulder or sirloin, cut
   into 1½-inch cubes
2 tablespoons vegetable oil
2 cups chopped onions
1 cup chopped green bell
   pepper
2 cloves garlic, minced
¼ cup chopped fresh
   cilantro
3 to 4 tablespoons chili
   powder
2 teaspoons dried oregano
   leaves
1 teaspoon salt
½ teaspoon crushed red
   pepper
2 cans (14½ ounces each)
   chicken broth
3 cups cubed, peeled
   potatoes, cut in 1-inch
   pieces
2 cups fresh or frozen
   whole kernel corn
1 can (16 ounces) garbanzo
   beans, drained**

Heat oil in Dutch oven. Brown
pork over medium-high heat.
Stir in onions, bell pepper,
garlic, cilantro, chili powder,
oregano, salt, red pepper and
chicken broth.

Cover; cook over medium-low
heat 45 to 55 minutes or until
pork is tender. Add potatoes,
corn and beans. Cover; cook
15 to 20 minutes longer.
Makes 8 servings

Prep Time: 20 minutes
Cook Time: 60 minutes

*Favorite recipe from **National Pork
Producers Council***

Simmering or stewing
consists of first browning
the meat before covering
it with liquid and
simmering, covered,
until fork-tender.

7

Hot and Sour Soup

....

3 cans (about 14 ounces each) chicken broth
8 ounces boneless skinless chicken breasts, cut into ¼-inch-thick strips
1 cup shredded carrots
1 cup thinly sliced mushrooms
½ cup bamboo shoots, cut into matchstick-size strips
2 tablespoons rice wine vinegar or white wine vinegar
½ to ¾ teaspoon white pepper
¼ to ½ teaspoon hot pepper sauce
2 tablespoons cornstarch
2 tablespoons soy sauce
1 tablespoon dry sherry
2 medium green onions, sliced
1 egg, slightly beaten

Combine chicken broth, chicken, carrots, mushrooms, bamboo shoots, vinegar, pepper and hot pepper sauce in large saucepan. Bring to a boil over medium-high heat; reduce heat to low. Cover and simmer about 5 minutes or until chicken is no longer pink in center.

Stir together cornstarch, soy sauce and sherry in small bowl until smooth. Add to chicken broth mixture. Cook and stir until mixture comes to a boil. Stir in green onions and egg. Cook about 1 minute, stirring in one direction, until egg is cooked. Ladle soup into bowls.
Makes 6 side-dish servings

Hot and Sour Soup

Southwestern Beef Stew

¼ cup all-purpose flour
1 teaspoon salt
1 teaspoon chili powder
1 teaspoon ground cumin
1 pound lean beef stew meat, cut into 1-inch cubes*
2 teaspoons vegetable oil
1 large onion, cut into chunks
2 teaspoons fresh or bottled minced garlic
1 can (about 14 ounces) reduced-sodium beef broth
½ cup prepared salsa or picante sauce
12 ounces red potatoes, cut into 1-inch chunks
1 cup (4 ounces) baby carrots
2 green or yellow bell peppers (or 1 of each), cut into 1-inch chunks
¼ cup chopped fresh cilantro

*If lean stew meat is not available, choose lean top round steak or chuck steak, trim it and cut it into cubes.

1. Place flour and seasonings in large resealable plastic food storage bag. Add beef; shake to coat. Heat oil in large deep nonstick skillet or Dutch oven over medium heat until hot. Remove beef from bag, reserving remaining flour mixture. Add beef to skillet; brown on all sides, about 5 minutes. Remove and set aside.

2. Add onion and garlic to same skillet. Cook 5 minutes over medium heat, stirring occasionally. Sprinkle reserved flour mixture over onion mixture; cook and stir 1 minute. Add beef broth and salsa; bring to a boil. Return beef and any accumulated juices to skillet. Reduce heat; cover and simmer over low heat 40 minutes.

3. Stir in potatoes, carrots and bell peppers. Cover; simmer 35 to 40 minutes or until beef and vegetables are tender. Sprinkle with cilantro.
    Makes 6 (1¼-cup) servings

Note: Substitute 1 tablespoon Mexican seasoning for mixture of salt, chili powder and cumin, if desired.

Prep Time: 20 minutes
Cook Time: 1 hour 20 minutes

Mexican Hot Pot

....

1 tablespoon canola oil
1 onion, sliced
3 cloves garlic, minced
2 teaspoons red pepper
    flakes
2 teaspoons dried oregano
    leaves, crushed
1 teaspoon ground cumin
1 can (28 ounces)
    tomatoes, chopped
1 can (15 ounces) chick-
    peas (garbanzo beans),
    rinsed and drained
1 can (15 ounces) pinto
    beans, rinsed and
    drained
2 cups whole kernel corn,
    fresh or frozen
1 cup water
6 cups shredded iceberg
    lettuce

1. Heat oil in stockpot or Dutch
oven over medium-high heat.
Add onion and garlic; cook and
stir 5 minutes. Add red pepper
flakes, oregano and cumin; mix
well.

2. Stir in tomatoes, chick-peas,
pinto beans, corn and water;
bring to a boil over high heat.

3. Reduce heat to medium-low;
cover and simmer 15 minutes.
Top individual servings with
1 cup shredded lettuce. Serve hot.
    Makes 6 servings

Hearty Buffalo-Style Vegetable Soup

....

2 cans (10½ ounces *each*)
    chicken or beef broth
3 tablespoons *Frank's®
    RedHot®* Sauce
1 bag (16 ounces) frozen
    vegetables
1½ cups diced cooked
    chicken or Polish
    sausage
6 thick slices French bread
3 tablespoons blue cheese,
    crumbled

1. Combine broth, *2½ cups
water* and *RedHot* Sauce in large
saucepan. Heat to boiling. Add
vegetables and chicken. Reduce
heat to medium-low. Cook,
covered, 7 minutes or until
vegetables are tender.

2. Preheat oven broiler. Toast
bread slightly on both sides. Top
one side with blue cheese. Place
under broiler until cheese is
melted and bread is crisp.

3. Ladle soup into warm bowls.
Top each bowl with 1 blue
cheese toast.   *Makes 6 servings*

Winter White Chili

....

½ pound boneless pork loin *or* 2 boneless pork chops, cut into ½-inch cubes

½ cup chopped onion

1 teaspoon vegetable oil

1 (16-ounce) can navy beans, drained

1 (16-ounce) can chick-peas, drained

1 (16-ounce) can white kernel corn, drained

1 (14½-ounce) can chicken broth

1 cup cooked wild rice

1 (4-ounce) can diced green chilies, drained

1½ teaspoons ground cumin

¼ teaspoon garlic powder

⅛ teaspoon hot pepper sauce

Chopped parsley

Shredded cheese

In 4-quart saucepan, sauté pork and onion in oil over medium-high heat until onion is soft and pork is lightly browned, about 5 minutes. Stir in remaining ingredients except parsley and cheese.

Cover and simmer for 20 minutes. Serve each portion garnished with parsley and cheese.   *Makes 6 servings*

Preparation Time: 10 minutes
Cooking Time: 25 minutes

*Favorite recipe from **National Pork Producers Council***

Wild rice is a cereal grain, but not a true rice. It has a nutty flavor and is higher in protein than white rice.

Spicy Pumpkin Soup with Green Chili Swirl

1 can (4 ounces) diced green chilies
¼ cup reduced-fat sour cream
¼ cup fresh cilantro leaves
1 can (15 ounces) solid-pack pumpkin
1 can (about 14 ounces) fat-free reduced-sodium chicken broth
½ cup water
1 teaspoon ground cumin
½ teaspoon chili powder
¼ teaspoon garlic powder
⅛ teaspoon ground red pepper (optional)
Additional sour cream (optional)

1. Combine green chilies, sour cream and cilantro in food processor or blender; process until smooth.*

2. Combine pumpkin, chicken broth, water, cumin, chili powder, garlic powder and red pepper, if desired, in medium saucepan; stir in ¼ cup green chili mixture. Bring to a boil; reduce heat to medium. Simmer, uncovered 5 minutes, stirring occasionally.

3. Pour into serving bowls. Top each serving with small dollops of remaining green chili mixture and additional sour cream, if desired. Run tip of spoon through dollops to swirl.

Makes 4 servings

*Omit food processor step by adding green chilies directly to soup. Finely chop cilantro and combine with sour cream. Dollop with sour cream-cilantro mixture as directed.

Spicy Pumpkin Soup with Green Chili Swirl

Spicy Shrimp Gumbo

....

½ cup vegetable oil
½ cup all-purpose flour
1 large onion, chopped
½ cup chopped fresh
    parsley
½ cup chopped celery
½ cup sliced green onions
6 cloves garlic, minced
4 cups chicken broth or
    water*
1 package (10 ounces)
    frozen sliced okra,
    thawed (optional)
1 teaspoon salt
½ teaspoon ground red
    pepper
2 pounds raw medium
    shrimp, peeled and
    deveined
3 cups hot cooked rice
    Fresh parsley sprigs for
    garnish

*Traditional gumbo's thickness is like stew. If you prefer it thinner, add 1 to 2 cups additional broth.

1. For roux, blend oil and flour in large heavy stockpot. Cook over medium heat 10 to 15 minutes or until roux is dark brown but not burned, stirring often.

2. Add onion, parsley, celery, green onions and garlic to roux. Cook over medium heat 5 to 10 minutes or until vegetables are tender. Add broth, okra, salt and red pepper. Cover; simmer 15 minutes.

3. Add shrimp; simmer 3 to 5 minutes or until shrimp turn pink and opaque.

4. Place about ⅓ cup rice into each wide-rimmed soup bowl; top with gumbo. Garnish, if desired.   *Makes 8 servings*

Spicy Shrimp Gumbo

7-Spice Chili with Corn Bread Topping

....

1 pound ground turkey <u>or</u> lean beef

1 jar (16 ounces) Original <u>or</u> Spicy TABASCO® brand 7-Spice Chili Recipe

1 can (16 ounces) kidney beans, rinsed and drained

¾ cup water

1 package (12 ounces) corn muffin mix

1 can (7 ounces) whole kernel corn with sweet green and red peppers, drained

1 cup (4 ounces) shredded Cheddar cheese

In large skillet, brown turkey; drain. Stir in TABASCO® 7-Spice Chili Recipe, beans and water. Bring to a boil; reduce heat. Simmer 10 minutes.

Divide evenly among 6 (12-ounce) individual ramekins.

Meanwhile, prepare corn muffin mix according to package directions. Stir in corn and cheese until well blended.

Pour about ½ cup muffin mixture over top of each ramekin. Bake at 400°F 15 minutes or until corn bread topping is golden brown.

Makes 6 servings

Classic Texas Chili

∙∙∙∙∙∙∙∙∙∙∙∙∙∙∙∙∙∙∙∙∙∙∙∙∙∙∙∙

¼ **cup vegetable oil**
3 **pounds beef round <u>or</u>
   chuck, cut into 1-inch
   cubes**
4 **to 6 tablespoons chili
   powder**
3 **cloves garlic, minced**
2 **teaspoons salt**
2 **teaspoons dried oregano
   leaves**
2 **teaspoons ground cumin**
2 **teaspoons TABASCO®
   brand Pepper Sauce**
1½ **quarts water**
⅓ **cup white cornmeal
   Chopped onion
   (optional)**

Heat oil in large saucepan over
medium high heat. Add beef
and brown on all sides. Stir in
chili powder, garlic, salt,
oregano, cumin, TABASCO®
Sauce and water; heat to boiling.
Reduce heat; cover and simmer
1¼ hours, stirring occasionally.
Add cornmeal and mix well.
Simmer, uncovered, 30 minutes
or until beef is tender. Garnish
with chopped onion, if desired.
Serve with rice and beans.

Makes 6 to 8 servings

Beef Steak Chili

∙∙∙∙∙∙∙∙∙∙∙∙∙∙∙∙∙∙∙∙∙∙∙∙∙∙∙∙∙

1 **pound beef steak**
2 **cans (14½ ounces each)
   DEL MONTE® Zesty
   Chili Style Chunky
   Tomatoes**
1 **can (15 ounces) black or
   kidney beans, rinsed
   and drained**
1 **can (8¾ ounces)
   DEL MONTE Whole
   Kernel Corn, drained**
2 **tablespoons fresh lime
   juice**

1. Season meat with garlic salt
and pepper. Grill over hot coals
(or broil) about 5 minutes on
each side or until desired
doneness. Cut into strips;
dice strips.

2. Cook tomatoes and beans in
large skillet over medium-high
heat 5 minutes or until slightly
thickened, stirring occasionally.

3. Stir in meat, corn and lime
juice; heat through. Season with
salt and pepper, if desired.

4. Sprinkle with chopped
cilantro, if desired.

Makes 4 servings

19

Spicy Sichuan Pork Stew

....

2 pounds boneless pork
   shoulder (Boston butt)
¼ cup all-purpose flour
2 tablespoons vegetable oil
1¾ cups water, divided
¼ cup KIKKOMAN® Soy
   Sauce
3 tablespoons dry sherry
2 cloves garlic, pressed
1 teaspoon minced fresh
   ginger root
½ teaspoon crushed red
   pepper
¼ teaspoon fennel seed,
   crushed
8 green onions and tops,
   cut into 1-inch
   lengths, separating
   whites from tops
2 large carrots, cut into
   chunks
   Hot cooked rice

Cut pork into 1-inch cubes. Coat in flour; reserve 2 tablespoons remaining flour. Heat oil in Dutch oven or large pan over medium-high heat; brown pork on all sides in hot oil. Add 1½ cups water, soy sauce, sherry, garlic, ginger, red pepper, fennel seed and white parts of green onions.

Cover pan; bring to a boil. Reduce heat and simmer 30 minutes. Add carrots; simmer, covered, 30 minutes longer, or until pork and carrots are tender. Meanwhile, combine reserved 2 tablespoons flour and remaining ¼ cup water; set aside. Stir green onion tops into pork mixture; simmer 1 minute. Add flour mixture; bring to a boil. Cook and stir until mixture is slightly thickened. Serve over rice. *Makes 6 servings*

Spicy Sichuan Pork Stew

Green Flash Turkey Chili

••••••••••••••••••••••••••••••

3 tablespoons olive oil, divided
3 large stalks celery, diced
1 large green bell pepper, diced
2 green onions, sliced
2 large cloves garlic, minced
1 pound ground turkey
4 cups canned white kidney beans, drained and rinsed
1½ cups water
⅓ cup TABASCO® brand Green Pepper Sauce
1¼ teaspoons salt
¼ cup chopped fresh parsley

Heat 2 tablespoons oil in large saucepan over medium heat. Add celery and green bell pepper; cook about 5 minutes or until crisp-tender. Add green onions and garlic; cook 5 minutes, stirring occasionally. Remove vegetables to plate with slotted spoon. Add remaining 1 tablespoon oil to saucepan; cook turkey over medium-high heat until well browned, stirring frequently.

Add vegetable mixture, kidney beans, water, TABASCO® Green Pepper Sauce and salt to saucepan. Heat to boiling over high heat. Reduce heat to low; cover and simmer 20 minutes, stirring occasionally. Uncover saucepan and simmer 5 minutes. Stir in parsley just before serving.

Makes 6 servings

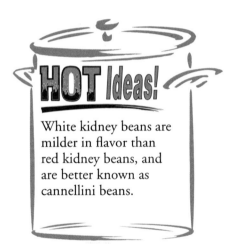

HOT Ideas!

White kidney beans are milder in flavor than red kidney beans, and are better known as cannellini beans.

Spicy Tomato Chili with Red Beans

• •

1 tablespoon olive oil
1 cup chopped green bell
   pepper
1 cup chopped onion
1 cup sliced celery
1 clove garlic, minced
1 can (15 ounces) diced
   tomatoes, undrained
1 can (15 ounces) red
   beans, drained and
   rinsed
1 can (10 ounces) diced
   tomatoes with green
   chilies
1 can (8 ounces) low-
   sodium tomato sauce
8 (6-inch) corn tortillas

1. Preheat oven to 400°F.

2. Heat oil in large saucepan over medium heat until hot. Add bell pepper, onion, celery and garlic. Cook and stir 5 minutes or until onion is translucent.

3. Add remaining ingredients except tortillas. Bring to a boil; reduce heat to low. Simmer 15 minutes. Cut each tortilla into 8 wedges. Place on baking sheet; bake 8 minutes or until crisp. Crush half of tortilla wedges; place in bottom of soup bowls. Spoon chili over tortillas. Serve with remaining tortilla wedges.   *Makes 4 servings*

Rice and Roast Beef Sandwiches

1 small red onion, sliced into thin rings
1 teaspoon olive oil
3 cups cooked brown rice
½ cup whole kernel corn
½ cup sliced ripe olives (optional)
½ cup barbecue sauce
2 tablespoons lime juice
½ teaspoon ground cumin
½ teaspoon garlic salt
4 whole-wheat pita rounds, halved and warmed
8 lettuce leaves
1 cup sliced, cooked lean roast beef
1 large tomato, seeded and chopped

Cook onion in oil in large skillet over medium-high heat until tender. Add rice, corn, olives, barbecue sauce, lime juice, cumin and garlic salt; toss until heated. Line each pita half with lettuce leaf, ½ cup hot rice mixture and roast beef; top with tomato.

Makes 8 (½ pita) sandwiches

Favorite recipe from USA Rice Federation

Bayou-Style Pot Pie

1 tablespoon olive oil
1 large onion, chopped
1 green bell pepper, chopped
1½ teaspoons minced garlic
8 ounces boneless skinless chicken thighs, cut into 1-inch pieces
1 can (14½ ounces) stewed tomatoes, undrained
8 ounces fully cooked smoked sausage, sliced
¾ teaspoon hot pepper sauce or to taste
2¼ cups buttermilk baking mix
¾ teaspoon dried thyme leaves
⅛ teaspoon black pepper
⅔ cup milk

1. Preheat oven to 450°F. Heat oil in medium ovenproof skillet over medium heat until hot. Add onion, bell pepper and garlic. Cook and stir 3 minutes. Add chicken; cook 1 minute. Add tomatoes with juice, sausage and hot pepper sauce. Cook, uncovered, 5 minutes.

2. Mix baking mix, thyme and black pepper. Stir in milk. Drop batter by tablespoonfuls over chicken mixture. Bake 14 minutes or until biscuits are golden and chicken mixture is bubbly.   *Makes 4 servings*

Rice and Roast Beef Sandwiches

It's Slow Good!

What's your hurry? Stay in, pull up a chair and warm up with these classic slow cooker recipes.

Tuscan Pasta

- 1 pound boneless skinless chicken breasts, cut into 1-inch pieces
- 1 can (15½ ounces) red kidney beans, rinsed and drained
- 1 can (15 ounces) tomato sauce
- 2 cans (14½ ounces each) Italian-style stewed tomatoes
- 1 jar (4½ ounces) sliced mushrooms, drained
- 1 medium green bell pepper, chopped
- ½ cup chopped onion
- ½ cup chopped celery
- 4 cloves garlic, minced
- 1 cup water
- 1 teaspoon dried Italian seasoning
- 6 ounces uncooked thin spaghetti, broken into halves

Place all ingredients except spaghetti in slow cooker. Cover and cook on LOW 4 hours or until vegetables are tender.

Turn to HIGH. Stir in spaghetti; cover. Stir again after 10 minutes. Cover and cook 45 minutes or until pasta is tender. Garnish with basil and bell pepper strips, if desired.   *Makes 8 servings*

Tuscan Pasta

Chicken and Vegetable Chowder

1 pound boneless skinless chicken breasts, cut into 1-inch pieces
10 ounces frozen broccoli cuts
1 cup sliced carrots
½ cup chopped onion
½ cup whole kernel corn
1 jar (4½ ounces) sliced mushrooms, drained
2 cloves garlic, minced
½ teaspoon dried thyme leaves
1 can (14½ ounces) reduced-sodium chicken broth
1 can (10¾ ounces) condensed cream of potato soup
⅓ cup half-and-half

Combine all ingredients except half-and-half in slow cooker. Cover and cook on LOW 5 hours or until vegetables are tender and chicken is no longer pink in center. Stir in half-and-half. Turn to HIGH. Cover and cook 15 minutes or until heated through. *Makes 6 servings*

Caponata

1 medium eggplant (about 1 pound), peeled and cut into ½-inch pieces
1 can (14½ ounces) diced Italian plum tomatoes, undrained
1 medium onion, chopped
1 red bell pepper, cut into ½-inch pieces
½ cup prepared medium-hot salsa
¼ cup extra-virgin olive oil
2 tablespoons capers, drained
2 tablespoons balsamic vinegar
3 cloves garlic, minced
1 teaspoon dried oregano leaves
¼ teaspoon salt
⅓ cup packed fresh basil, cut into thin strips
Toasted sliced Italian or French bread

Mix all ingredients except basil and bread in slow cooker. Cover and cook on LOW 7 to 8 hours or until vegetables are crisp-tender. Stir in basil. Serve at room temperature on toasted bread. *Makes about 5¼ cups*

Chicken and Vegetable Chowder

Favorite Beef Stew

. . . .

3 carrots, cut lengthwise
    into halves, then cut
    into 1-inch pieces
3 ribs celery, cut into
    1-inch pieces
2 large potatoes, peeled
    and cut into ½-inch
    pieces
1½ cups chopped onions
3 cloves garlic, chopped
1 bay leaf
4½ teaspoons Worcestershire
    sauce
¾ teaspoon dried thyme
    leaves
¾ teaspoon dried basil
    leaves
½ teaspoon black pepper
2 pounds lean beef stew
    meat, cut into 1-inch
    pieces
1 can (14½ ounces) diced
    tomatoes, undrained
1 can (about 14 ounces)
    reduced-sodium beef
    broth
½ cup cold water
¼ cup all-purpose flour

Layer ingredients in slow cooker
in the following order: carrots,
celery, potatoes, onions, garlic,
bay leaf, Worcestershire sauce,
thyme, basil, pepper, beef,
tomatoes with juice and broth.

Cover and cook on LOW 8 to
9 hours.

Remove beef and vegetables to
large serving bowl; cover and
keep warm. Remove and discard
bay leaf. Turn slow cooker to
HIGH; cover. Stir water into
flour in small bowl until smooth.
Add ½ cup cooking liquid;
mix well. Stir flour mixture into
slow cooker. Cover and cook
15 minutes or until thickened.
Pour sauce over meat and
vegetables. Serve immediately.
        Makes 6 to 8 servings

Favorite Beef Stew

Mediterranean Shrimp Soup

. . . .

1 medium onion, chopped
½ medium green bell
    pepper, chopped
2 cloves garlic, minced
1 can (14½ ounces) whole
    tomatoes, undrained
    and coarsely chopped
2 cans (14½ ounces each)
    reduced-sodium
    chicken broth
1 can (8 ounces) tomato
    sauce
1 jar (2½ ounces) sliced
    mushrooms
¼ cup ripe olives, sliced
½ cup orange juice
½ cup dry white wine
    (optional)
2 bay leaves
1 teaspoon dried basil
    leaves
¼ teaspoon fennel seed,
    crushed
⅛ teaspoon black pepper
1 pound medium shrimp,
    peeled

Place all ingredients except shrimp in slow cooker. Cover and cook on LOW 4 to 4½ hours or until vegetables are crisp-tender. Stir in shrimp.

Cover and cook 15 to 30 minutes or until shrimp are opaque. Remove and discard bay leaves.

Makes 6 servings

HOT Ideas!

For a heartier soup, add some fish. Cut 1 pound of whitefish or cod into 1-inch pieces. Add fish to your slow cooker 45 minutes before serving. Cover and cook on low.

Mediterranean Shrimp Soup

Minestrone alla Milanese

- 2 cans (14½ ounces each) reduced-sodium beef broth
- 1 can (14½ ounces) diced tomatoes, undrained
- 1 cup diced potato
- 1 cup coarsely chopped green cabbage
- 1 cup coarsely chopped carrots
- 1 cup sliced zucchini
- ¾ cup chopped onion
- ¾ cup sliced fresh green beans
- ¾ cup coarsely chopped celery
- ¾ cup water
- 2 tablespoons olive oil
- 1 clove garlic, minced
- ½ teaspoon dried basil leaves
- ¼ teaspoon dried rosemary leaves
- 1 bay leaf
- 1 can (15½ ounces) cannellini beans, rinsed and drained
- Grated Parmesan cheese (optional)

Combine all ingredients except cannellini beans and cheese in slow cooker; mix well.

Cover and cook on LOW 5 to 6 hours. Add cannellini beans. Cover and cook on LOW 1 hour or until vegetables are crisp-tender. Remove and discard bay leaf. Garnish with cheese, if desired.

Makes 8 to 10 servings

Minestrone alla Milanese

Southwest Turkey Tenderloin Stew

....

1 package (about
   1½ pounds) turkey
   tenderloins, cut into
   ¾-inch pieces
1 tablespoon chili powder
1 teaspoon ground cumin
¼ teaspoon salt
1 red bell pepper, cut into
   ¾-inch pieces
1 green bell pepper, cut
   into ¾-inch pieces
¾ cup chopped red or
   yellow onion
3 cloves garlic, minced
1 can (15½ ounces) chili
   beans in spicy sauce,
   undrained
1 can (14½ ounces) chili-
   style stewed tomatoes,
   undrained
¾ cup prepared salsa or
   picante sauce
   Fresh cilantro (optional)

Place turkey in slow cooker. Sprinkle chili powder, cumin and salt over turkey; toss to coat. Add red bell pepper, green bell pepper, onion, garlic, beans, tomatoes and salsa. Mix well. Cover and cook on LOW 5 hours or until turkey is no longer pink in center and vegetables are crisp-tender. Ladle into bowls. Garnish with cilantro, if desired.

Makes 6 servings

HOT Ideas!

Like beef and pork tenderloin, turkey tenderloin is very lean and has significantly less fat than the leg and thigh portions.

Southwest Turkey Tenderloin Stew

Risi Bisi

1½ cups converted long-grain white rice
¾ cup chopped onion
2 cloves garlic, minced
2 cans (about 14 ounces each) reduced-sodium chicken broth
⅓ cup water
¾ teaspoon dried Italian seasoning
½ teaspoon dried basil leaves
½ cup frozen peas, thawed
¼ cup grated Parmesan cheese
¼ cup toasted pine nuts (optional)

Combine rice, onion and garlic in slow cooker. Heat broth and water in small saucepan to a boil. Stir boiling liquid, Italian seasoning and basil into rice mixture.

Cover and cook on LOW 2 to 3 hours or until liquid is absorbed. Add peas. Cover and cook 1 hour. Stir in cheese. Spoon rice into serving bowl. Sprinkle with pine nuts, if desired. *Makes 6 servings*

Rustic Potatoes au Gratin

½ cup milk
1 can (10¾ ounces) condensed Cheddar cheese soup, undiluted
1 package (8 ounces) cream cheese, softened
1 clove garlic, minced
¼ teaspoon ground nutmeg
⅛ teaspoon black pepper
2 pounds baking potatoes, cut into ¼-inch slices
1 small onion, thinly sliced
Paprika (optional)

Heat milk in small saucepan over medium heat until small bubbles form around edge of pan. Remove from heat. Add soup, cream cheese, garlic, nutmeg and pepper. Stir until smooth. Layer ¼ of potatoes and ¼ of onion in bottom of slow cooker. Top with ¼ of soup mixture. Repeat layers 3 times, using remaining potatoes, onion and soup mixture. Cover and cook on LOW 6½ to 7 hours or until potatoes are tender and most of liquid is absorbed. Sprinkle with paprika, if desired. *Makes 6 servings*

Broccoli and Beef Pasta

....

2 cups broccoli florets *or*
    1 package (10 ounces)
    frozen broccoli,
    thawed
1 onion, thinly sliced
½ teaspoon dried basil
    leaves
½ teaspoon dried oregano
    leaves
½ teaspoon dried thyme
    leaves
1 can (14½ ounces) Italian-
    style diced tomatoes,
    undrained
¾ cup beef broth
1 pound lean ground beef
2 cloves garlic, minced
2 tablespoons tomato paste
2 cups cooked rotini pasta
3 ounces shredded
    Cheddar cheese or
    grated Parmesan
    cheese

SLOW COOKER DIRECTIONS

Layer broccoli, onion, basil, oregano, thyme, tomatoes with juice and beef broth in slow cooker. Cover and cook on LOW 2½ hours.

Combine beef and garlic in large nonstick skillet; cook over high heat 6 to 8 minutes or until meat is no longer pink, breaking meat apart with wooden spoon. Pour off drippings. Add beef mixture to slow cooker. Cover and cook 2 hours.

Stir in tomato paste. Add pasta and cheese. Cover and cook 30 minutes or until cheese melts and mixture is heated through. Sprinkle with additional shredded cheese, if desired.

Makes 4 servings

Serving Suggestion: Serve with garlic bread.

Coq au Vin

....

4 slices thick-cut bacon

2 cups frozen pearl onions, thawed

1 cup sliced button mushrooms

1 clove garlic, minced

1 teaspoon dried thyme leaves

⅛ teaspoon black pepper

6 boneless skinless chicken breast halves (about 2 pounds)

½ cup dry red wine

¾ cup reduced-sodium chicken broth

¼ cup tomato paste

3 tablespoons all-purpose flour

Cook bacon in medium skillet over medium heat. Drain and crumble. Layer ingredients in slow cooker in the following order: onions, bacon, mushrooms, garlic, thyme, pepper, chicken, wine and broth. Cover and cook on LOW 6 to 8 hours.

Remove chicken and vegetables; cover and keep warm. Ladle ½ cup cooking liquid into small bowl; allow to cool slightly. Turn slow cooker to HIGH; cover.

Mix reserved liquid, tomato paste and flour until smooth. Return mixture to slow cooker; cover and cook 15 minutes or until thickened. Serve over egg noodles, if desired.

Makes 6 servings

This classic French dish originated when farmers needed a way to cook old chickens that could no longer breed. A slow, moist cooking method was needed to tenderize the tough old birds.

Coq au Vin

Hearty Flavors

Fill your bowl to the rim with these stick-to-your-ribs favorites.

Hearty Tortellini Soup

··

- **1 small red onion, chopped**
- **2 medium carrots, chopped**
- **2 ribs celery, thinly sliced**
- **1 small zucchini, chopped**
- **2 plum tomatoes, chopped**
- **2 cloves garlic, minced**
- **2 cans (14½ ounces *each*) chicken broth**
- **1 can (15 to 19 ounces) red kidney beans, rinsed and drained**
- **2 tablespoons *French's®* Worcestershire Sauce**
- **1 package (9 ounces) refrigerated tortellini pasta**

1. Heat *2 tablespoons oil* in 6-quart saucepot or Dutch oven over medium-high heat. Add vegetables, tomatoes and garlic. Cook and stir 5 minutes or until vegetables are crisp-tender.

2. Add broth, *½ cup water,* beans and Worcestershire. Heat to boiling. Stir in pasta. Return to boiling. Cook 5 minutes or until pasta is tender, stirring occasionally. Serve with crusty bread and grated Parmesan cheese, if desired.

Makes 4 servings

Hearty Tortellini Soup

Manhattan Clam Chowder

....

¼ cup chopped bacon
1 cup chopped onion
½ cup chopped carrots
½ cup chopped celery
2 cans (14.5 ounces each)
   CONTADINA® Recipe
   Ready Diced Tomatoes,
   undrained
1 can (8 ounces)
   CONTADINA®
   Tomato Sauce
1 bottle (8 ounces) clam
   juice
1 large bay leaf
½ teaspoon chopped fresh
   rosemary
⅛ teaspoon pepper
2 cans (6.5 ounces each)
   chopped clams,
   undrained

1. Sauté bacon with onion, carrots and celery in large saucepan.

2. Stir in undrained tomatoes with remaining ingredients, except clams. Heat to boiling. Reduce heat; boil gently 15 minutes. Stir in clams and juice.

3. Heat additional 5 minutes. Remove bay leaf before serving.

Makes 6½ cups

Microwave Directions:
Combine bacon, onion, carrots and celery in 2-quart microwave-safe casserole dish. Microwave on HIGH (100%) power 5 minutes. Stir in remaining ingredients, except clams. Microwave on HIGH (100%) power 5 minutes. Stir in clams and juice. Microwave on HIGH (100%) power 5 minutes. Remove bay leaf before serving.

Stir-Fry Beef & Vegetable Soup

1 pound boneless beef steak, such as sirloin or round steak

2 teaspoons dark sesame oil, divided

3 cans (about 14 ounces each) reduced-sodium beef broth

1 package (16 ounces) frozen stir-fry vegetables

3 green onions, thinly sliced

¼ cup stir-fry sauce

1. Slice beef across grain into ⅛-inch-thick strips; cut strips into bite-size pieces.

2. Heat Dutch oven over high heat. Add 1 teaspoon oil and tilt pan to coat bottom. Add half the beef in single layer; cook 1 minute, without stirring, until slightly browned on bottom. Turn and brown other side about 1 minute. Remove beef from pan with slotted spoon; set aside. Repeat with remaining 1 teaspoon oil and beef; set aside.

3. Add broth to Dutch oven; cover and bring to a boil over high heat. Add vegetables; reduce heat to medium-high and simmer 3 to 5 minutes or until heated through. Add beef, green onions and stir-fry sauce; simmer 1 minute.

Makes 6 servings

Serving Suggestion: Make a quick sesame bread to serve with this soup. Brush refrigerated dinner roll dough with water, then dip in sesame seeds before baking.

Prep/Cook Time: 22 minutes

Chunky Beef Chili

- 2 tablespoons vegetable oil
- 2½ pounds boneless beef chuck, cut into ½-inch pieces
- 1 cup coarsely chopped onion
- 1 cup chopped green bell pepper
- 2 cloves garlic, minced
- 1 teaspoon salt
- 1 can (28 ounces) Italian-style plum tomatoes, broken up and undrained
- 1 cup water
- 1 can (6 ounces) tomato paste
- 3 tablespoons chili powder
- 1 teaspoon dried oregano leaves
- ¼ to ½ teaspoon red pepper flakes
- 1 can (15½ ounces) red kidney beans, drained
- 6 tablespoons shredded sharp Cheddar cheese
- 6 tablespoons chopped onion

Heat oil in large skillet or Dutch oven over medium-high heat. Add boneless beef chuck pieces, 1 cup chopped onion, bell pepper and garlic; cook until beef is evenly browned.

Pour off drippings. Sprinkle salt over beef mixture. Add tomatoes with juice, water, tomato paste, chili powder, oregano and red pepper flakes. Cover tightly; reduce heat and simmer 1½ hours or until beef is tender. Add beans; continue cooking, uncovered, 20 to 30 minutes. Serve with cheese and additional chopped onion.

Makes 8 servings

*Favorite recipe from **National Cattlemen's Beef Association***

Chunky Beef Chili

Five-Way Cincinnati Chili

....

1 pound uncooked
     spaghetti
1 pound ground chuck
2 cans (10 ounces each)
     tomatoes and green
     chilies, undrained
1 can (15 ounces) red
     kidney beans, drained
1 can (10½ ounces)
     condensed French
     onion soup
1¼ cups water
1 tablespoon chili powder
1 teaspoon sugar
½ teaspoon salt
¼ teaspoon cinnamon
½ cup (2 ounces) shredded
     Cheddar cheese
½ cup chopped onion

Cook pasta according to package directions; drain. Brown beef in large saucepan over medium-high heat, stirring to separate; drain. Add tomatoes with liquid, beans, soup, water, chili powder, sugar, salt and cinnamon to saucepan; bring to a boil. Reduce heat to low. Simmer, uncovered, 10 minutes, stirring occasionally. Serve chili over hot spaghetti; sprinkle with cheese and onion.   *Makes 6 servings*

Oyster Stew

....

1 quart shucked oysters,
     with their liquor
8 cups milk
8 tablespoons margarine,
     cut into pieces
1 teaspoon freshly ground
     white pepper
½ teaspoon salt
     Paprika
2 tablespoons finely
     chopped fresh parsley

Heat oysters in their liquor in medium saucepan over high heat until oyster edges begin to curl, about 2 to 3 minutes. Heat milk and margarine together in large saucepan over medium-high heat just to boiling. Add pepper and salt.

Stir in oysters and their liquor. Do not boil or overcook stew or oysters may get tough. Pour stew into tureen. Dust with paprika; sprinkle with parsley.
     Makes 8 servings

Favorite recipe from National Fisheries Institute

Curried Turkey Stew with Dumplings

....

2 pounds turkey thighs
1 medium onion, chopped
4¾ cups cold water, divided
1 teaspoon salt
1 teaspoon dried thyme
   leaves
⅛ teaspoon black pepper
¼ cup cornstarch
1 teaspoon curry powder
2 cups frozen mixed
   vegetables, such as
   broccoli, cauliflower
   and carrots
1 large tart apple, peeled,
   cored and chopped
¾ cup all-purpose flour
1 tablespoon chopped fresh
   parsley
1¼ teaspoons baking powder
¼ teaspoon onion salt
2 tablespoons shortening
¼ cup milk
   Paprika
¼ cup chopped peanuts

Rinse turkey. Place onion, turkey, 4 cups water, salt, thyme and pepper in 5-quart Dutch oven. Bring to a boil over high heat. Reduce heat to medium-low; simmer, uncovered, 1 hour 45 minutes or until turkey is tender.

Remove turkey from soup and let cool slightly. Skim fat from soup. Remove turkey meat from bones; discard skin and bones. Cut turkey into bite-size pieces.

Stir together remaining ¾ cup cold water, cornstarch and curry in small bowl until smooth. Stir into broth. Cook and stir over medium heat until mixture comes to a boil and thickens. Stir in frozen vegetables, turkey pieces and apple. Bring to a boil over high heat, stirring often.

For dumplings, stir together flour, parsley, baking powder, and onion salt. Cut in shortening until mixture forms pea-sized pieces. Stir in milk until just combined.

Drop dough in six mounds on stew. Cover and simmer over medium-low heat about 15 minutes or until toothpick inserted in centers of dumplings comes out clean.

Sprinkle dumplings with paprika. Spoon stew into bowls placing dumpling on top of each serving; sprinkle with peanuts. Garnish, if desired.
Makes 6 servings

Chicken & Orzo Soup

Nonstick cooking spray
3 ounces boneless skinless chicken breast, cut into bite-size pieces
1 can (about 14 ounces) fat-free, reduced-sodium chicken broth
1 cup water
⅔ cup shredded carrot
⅓ cup sliced green onion
¼ cup uncooked orzo pasta
1 teaspoon grated fresh ginger
⅛ teaspoon ground turmeric
2 teaspoons lemon juice
Black pepper
Sliced green onions (optional)

1. Spray medium saucepan with cooking spray. Heat over medium-high heat until hot. Add chicken. Cook and stir 2 to 3 minutes or until no longer pink. Remove from saucepan and set aside.

2. In same saucepan combine broth, water, carrot, onion, orzo, ginger and turmeric. Bring to a boil. Reduce heat and simmer, covered, 8 to 10 minutes or until orzo is tender. Stir in chicken and lemon juice; cook until hot. Season to taste with pepper.

3. Ladle into serving bowls. Sprinkle with green onions, if desired. *Makes 2 servings*

The word "orzo" actually means barley, even though the shape of this pasta looks more like rice. You can find it in most large supermarkets.

French Beef Stew

1½ pounds stew beef, cut into 1-inch cubes
¼ cup all-purpose flour
2 tablespoons vegetable oil
2 cans (14½ ounces each) DEL MONTE® Diced Tomatoes with Garlic & Onion
1 can (14 ounces) beef broth
4 medium carrots, peeled and cut into 1-inch chunks
2 medium potatoes, peeled and cut into 1-inch chunks
¾ teaspoon dried thyme, crushed
2 tablespoons Dijon mustard (optional)

1. Combine meat and flour in large plastic food storage bag; toss to coat evenly.

2. Brown meat in hot oil in 6-quart saucepan. Season with salt and pepper, if desired.

3. Add all remaining ingredients except mustard. Bring to boil; reduce heat to medium-low. Cover; simmer 1 hour or until beef is tender.

4. Blend in mustard. Garnish and serve with warm crusty French bread, if desired.

Makes 6 to 8 servings

Prep Time: 10 minutes
Cook Time: 1 hour

French Beef Stew

Easy Creole Chicken and Zucchini

Vegetable cooking spray
4 chicken quarters
1 medium onion, chopped
¼ cup chopped green bell pepper
2 cans (14½ ounces each) stewed tomatoes, undrained
1 pound zucchini, chopped (about 3 medium)
¼ cup dry sherry
1 bay leaf
1 teaspoon celery salt
½ teaspoon ground black pepper
½ teaspoon curry powder
¼ teaspoon dried basil
4 cups hot cooked rice

Heat large Dutch oven coated with cooking spray over medium-high heat until hot. Add chicken. Cook about 10 minutes or until brown, turning occasionally. Remove chicken from pan; spoon off fat. Add onion and green pepper to pan; cook 5 minutes or until onion is tender. Stir in tomatoes and juice, zucchini, sherry, bay leaf, celery salt, black pepper, curry and basil.

Arrange chicken over tomato mixture; cover and simmer over medium-low heat 30 minutes or until fork can be inserted into chicken with ease and juices run clear, not pink. Remove bay leaf. Serve over hot rice.

Makes 4 servings

Favorite recipe from USA Rice Federation

Creole cooking is a hearty blend of French, Spanish and African cuisines. New Orleans is well known for authentic Creole cooking.

Hearty Lentil Stew

·····································

2 tablespoons olive or
vegetable oil
3 medium carrots, sliced
3 ribs celery, sliced
1 cup lentils
3 cups water, divided
1 envelope LIPTON®
RECIPE SECRETS®
Savory Herb with
Garlic Soup Mix*
1 tablespoon cider vinegar
or red wine vinegar
Hot cooked brown rice,
couscous or pasta

*Also terrific with Lipton® Recipe
Secrets® Onion-Mushroom or
Onion Soup Mix.

In 3-quart saucepan, heat oil
over medium heat and cook
carrots and celery, stirring
occasionally, 3 minutes. Add
lentils and cook 1 minute. Stir
in 2 cups water. Bring to a boil
over high heat. Reduce heat to
low and simmer covered, stirring
occasionally, 25 minutes. Stir
in savory herb with garlic soup
mix blended with remaining
1 cup water. Simmer covered
additional 10 minutes or until
lentils are tender. Stir in vinegar.
Serve over hot rice.

Makes about 4 servings

Ham and Beer Cheese Soup

·····································

1 cup chopped onion
½ cup sliced celery
2 tablespoons butter or
margarine
1 cup hot water
1 HERB-OX® chicken
flavor bouillon cube or
1 teaspoon instant
chicken bouillon
3 cups half-and-half
3 cups (18 ounces) diced
CURE 81® ham
1 (16-ounce) loaf
pasteurized process
cheese spread, cubed
1 (12-ounce) can beer
3 tablespoons all-purpose
flour
Popcorn (optional)

In Dutch oven over medium-
high heat, sauté onion and
celery in butter until tender. In
small liquid measuring cup,
combine water and bouillon; set
aside. Add half-and-half, ham,
cheese, beer and ¾ cup broth to
onion and celery mixture.
Cook, stirring constantly, until
cheese melts. Combine
remaining ¼ cup broth and
flour; stir until smooth. Add
flour mixture to soup, stirring
constantly. Cook, stirring
constantly, until slightly
thickened. Sprinkle individual
servings with popcorn, if
desired.   *Makes 8 servings*

Ham and Broccoli Chowder

· ·

2 cups broccoli florets
1 cup chopped onion
2 ribs celery, sliced
¼ cup water
½ cup all-purpose flour
3 cups skim milk
1 teaspoon salt-free Italian
herb blend
¼ teaspoon black pepper
3 ounces 97% fat-free ham
½ cup (2 ounces) shredded
reduced-fat sharp
Cheddar cheese
5 green onions, chopped

1. Combine broccoli, onion, celery and water in 2-quart microwavable container. Cover and microwave at HIGH 6 minutes, stirring halfway through cooking.

2. Whisk together flour, milk, herb blend and pepper in medium bowl. Stir into vegetables. Cover and microwave at HIGH 6 minutes or until mixture thickens and comes to a boil, stirring every 2 minutes.

3. Cut ham into ½-inch pieces. Add ham to broccoli mixture. Cover and microwave at HIGH 1 minute. Add cheese. Cover and let stand 5 minutes. Stir until cheese is melted. To serve, ladle into and sprinkle with green onions.

Makes 4 (1½-cup) servings

Prep/Cook Time: 27 minutes

Ham and Broccoli Chowder

Lamb Meatball & Bean Soup

....

1 pound ground lamb
¼ cup chopped onion
1 clove garlic, minced
1 teaspoon ground cumin
½ teaspoon salt
2 cups chicken broth
1 (10-ounce) package
    frozen chopped
    broccoli*
1 large tomato, chopped
1 (15-ounce) can garbanzo
    beans or black-eyed
    peas, drained
½ teaspoon dried thyme
    leaves, crushed
Salt and pepper

*Substitute 1½ cups fresh broccoli florets for 10-ounce package frozen chopped broccoli.

Combine lamb, onion, garlic, cumin and salt; mix lightly. Shape into 1-inch balls.** Brown meatballs in large skillet over medium-high heat, turning occasionally.

Meanwhile, bring broth to a boil in large saucepan. Add broccoli and tomato; return to a boil. Reduce heat; cover.

When meatballs are browned, remove from skillet with slotted spoon. Add to broth with beans and thyme; simmer 5 minutes. Season to taste with salt and pepper.   *Makes 4 to 6 servings*

**To quickly shape uniform meatballs, place meat mixture on cutting board; pat evenly into large square, one inch thick. With sharp knife, cut meat into 1-inch squares; shape each square into a ball.

HOT Ideas!

Come and get it!
Want more great recipes?
We're on the Web!
Visit us today at
http://www.fbnr.com

Turkey, Corn and Sweet Potato Soup

....

- ½ cup chopped onion
- 1 small jalapeño pepper, minced
- 1 teaspoon margarine
- 5 cups turkey broth or reduced sodium chicken bouillon
- 1½ pounds sweet potatoes, peeled and cut into 1-inch cubes
- 2 cups cooked turkey, cut into ½-inch cubes
- ½ teaspoon salt
- 1½ cups frozen corn
  Fresh cilantro (optional)

In 5-quart saucepan, over medium-high heat, cook and stir onion and jalapeño pepper in margarine 5 minutes or until onion is soft. Add broth, potatoes, turkey and salt; bring to a boil. Reduce heat to low, cover and simmer 20 to 25 minutes or until potatoes are tender. Stir in corn. Increase heat to medium and cook 5 to 6 minutes.

To serve, spoon 1 cup soup in bowl and garnish with cilantro, if desired.   *Makes 8 servings*

Favorite recipe from National Turkey Federation

Veg•All® Black Bean Soup

....

- 1 package (14 ounces) smoked sausage, cut into ½-inch slices
- 2 cans (15 ounces each) VEG•ALL® Original Mixed Vegetables
- 2 cans (15 ounces each) black beans with spices
- 1 can (14½ ounces) chicken broth

In large soup kettle, lightly brown sausage. Add Veg•All, beans, and chicken broth; heat until hot. Serve immediately.
          Makes 4 to 6 servings

From the Garden

Satisfy your appetite with this enchanting selection of meals that are bursting with vegetables.

Middle Eastern Lentil Soup

1 cup dried lentils
2 tablespoons olive oil
1 onion, chopped
1 red bell pepper, chopped
½ teaspoon ground cumin
1 teaspoon fennel seed
¼ teaspoon ground red
    pepper
4 cups water
½ teaspoon salt
1 tablespoon lemon juice
½ cup plain low-fat yogurt
2 tablespoons chopped
    fresh parsley

1. Rinse lentils, discarding any debris or blemished lentils; drain.

2. Heat oil in large saucepan over medium-high heat until hot. Add onion and bell pepper; cook and stir 5 minutes or until tender. Add cumin, fennel seed and ground red pepper; cook and stir 1 minute.

3. Add water and lentils. Bring to a boil. Reduce heat to low. Cover and simmer 20 minutes. Stir in salt. Simmer 5 to 10 minutes more or until lentils are tender. Stir in lemon juice.

4. To serve, ladle soup into bowls and top with yogurt; sprinkle with parsley.

Makes 4 servings

Middle Eastern Lentil Soup

Minute-Minestrone with Bays® Crostini

2 cans (15 ounces each)
    country vegetable soup
2 leaves Romaine lettuce,
    chopped
2 slices prosciutto,
    chopped (optional)
½ medium zucchini, sliced
2 tablespoons grated
    Asiago cheese
1 cup leftover cooked pasta
    Olive oil
4 teaspoons prepared pesto
    Chopped Italian parsley
    Grated lemon rind
    BAYS® Crostini (recipe
    follows)

In a large saucepan, combine soup, Romaine, prosciutto, zucchini and cheese. Heat over low heat, stirring occasionally, until hot and bubbly. In a skillet or microwave, toss pasta with oil to heat thoroughly. Ladle soup into individual bowls. Stir one teaspoonful of prepared pesto into each serving. Spoon pasta on top; sprinkle with parsley and lemon rind. Serve with Bays® Crostini.

Makes 4 servings

Other additions: Leftover cooked sugar snap peas or green beans, cut up; pepperoni or chopped ham.

Bays® Crostini

2 tablespoons olive oil
1 teaspoon dry Italian
    salad dressing mix
4 BAYS® English muffins,
    split
2 tablespoons grated
    Asiago cheese
1 tablespoon grated
    Romano cheese

Combine oil and dressing mix; brush on both sides of muffin halves. Place on baking sheet. Bake in a preheated 325°F oven for 15 minutes. Remove from oven; sprinkle with cheeses. Serve warm or at room temperature.

Cheesy Vegetable Soup

2 teaspoons CRICSO® Oil*
¼ cup chopped green or red bell pepper
¼ cup chopped onion
2 tablespoons all-purpose flour
½ teaspoon dry mustard
⅛ teaspoon cayenne pepper
1 cup chicken broth
½ cup skim milk
1 package (10 ounces) mixed vegetables (broccoli, cauliflower and carrots) in cheese flavor sauce, thawed
1 package (9 ounces) frozen cut green beans, thawed

*Use your favorite Crisco Oil product.

1. Heat oil in large saucepan on medium heat. Add green pepper and onion. Cook and stir 2 to 3 minutes or until crisp-tender. Remove from heat.

2. Stir in flour, dry mustard and cayenne. Stir in broth and milk gradually. Return to heat. Cook and stir until mixture thickens.

3. Stir in vegetables in cheese sauce and green beans. Simmer 5 minutes or until vegetables are tender. *Makes 4 servings*

Southwestern Two Bean Chili & Rice

1 bag (about ½ cup uncooked) boil-in-bag white rice
1 tablespoon vegetable oil
1 cup chopped onion
1 cup chopped green bell pepper
1½ teaspoons bottled minced garlic
1 can (15½ ounces) chili beans in spicy or mild sauce, undrained
1 can (15½ ounces) black or pinto beans, drained
1 can (10 ounces) diced tomatoes with green chilies, undrained
1 tablespoon chili powder
2 teaspoons ground cumin
1 cup (4 ounces) shredded Cheddar or Monterey Jack cheese

1. Cook rice according to package directions.

2. While rice is cooking, heat oil in large saucepan over medium-high heat until hot. Add onion, bell pepper and garlic. Cook 5 minutes, stirring occasionally. Stir in chili beans with sauce, black beans, tomatoes with juice, chili powder and cumin. Cover; bring to a boil over high heat. Reduce heat to medium-low. Simmer, covered, 10 minutes.

3. Transfer rice to 4 shallow bowls. Ladle bean mixture over rice; top with cheese.

Makes 4 servings

Prep/Cook Time: 20 minutes

Southwestern Two Bean Chili & Rice

Creamy Carrot Soup

3 cups water
4 cups sliced carrots
½ cup chopped onion
2 tablespoons packed
    brown sugar
2 teaspoons curry powder
2 cloves garlic, minced
⅛ teaspoon ground ginger
    Dash ground cinnamon
½ chicken flavor bouillon
    cube
½ cup skim milk

In large saucepan, bring water to a boil. Add remaining ingredients except milk. Reduce heat to low; simmer 40 minutes or until carrots are tender. Remove from heat; pour mixture in batches into food processor or blender. Process until smooth. Return mixture to saucepan. Over low heat, stir in milk, heating until warm but not boiling. Serve warm.

Makes 6 servings

Favorite recipe from **The Sugar Association, Inc.**

Tasty Vegetarian Chili

2 cans (15 ounces each)
    dark red kidney beans,
    drained
2 cans (14½ ounces each)
    diced tomatoes
1 can (6 ounces) tomato
    paste
1 small onion, chopped
3 tablespoons MRS. DASH®
    Garlic & Herb
    Seasoning
4 teaspoons sugar
1 tablespoon MRS. DASH®
    Extra Spicy Seasoning
1 tablespoon ground
    cumin
    Grated cheese (optional)

In medium saucepan, combine all ingredients, except cheese. Simmer over medium heat 5 to 10 minutes. Garnish with grated cheese, if desired.

Makes 8 servings

Cheesy Spinach Soup

¼ cup chopped onion
1 tablespoon reduced calorie margarine
2 cups skim milk
¾ pound (12 ounces) VELVEETA LIGHT® Pasteurized Prepared Cheese Product, cut up
1 package (10 ounces) frozen chopped spinach, cooked, well drained
⅛ teaspoon ground nutmeg
Dash pepper

1. Cook and stir onion in reduced calorie margarine in 2-quart saucepan until tender.

2. Add remaining ingredients; stir on low heat until Velveeta Light is melted and mixture is thoroughly heated.
Makes 4 (1-cup) servings

Prep Time: 5 minutes
Cook Time: 10 minutes

Wild Rice Soup

½ cup lentils
3 cups water
1 package (6 ounces) long grain and wild rice blend
1 can (about 14 ounces) vegetable broth
1 package (10 ounces) frozen mixed vegetables
1 cup fat-free (skim) milk
½ cup (2 ounces) reduced-fat processed American cheese, cut into pieces

1. Rinse and sort lentils, discarding any debris or blemished lentils. Combine lentils and water in small saucepan. Bring to a boil; reduce heat to low. Simmer, covered, 5 minutes. Let stand, covered, 1 hour. Drain and rinse lentils.

2. Cook rice according to package directions in medium saucepan. Add lentils and remaining ingredients. Bring to a boil; reduce heat to low. Simmer, uncovered, 20 minutes. Garnish as desired.
Makes 6 servings

Barley Stew with Cornmeal-Cheese Dumplings

....

2 cans (11½ ounces each) no-salt-added spicy vegetable juice cocktail
1 can (15½ ounces) butter beans, drained
1 can (14½ ounces) stewed tomatoes, undrained
1 cup sliced zucchini
1 cup sliced carrots
1 cup water
½ cup chopped peeled parsnip
⅓ cup quick pearl barley
1 bay leaf
2 tablespoons chopped fresh thyme
1½ tablespoons chopped fresh rosemary
⅓ cup all-purpose flour
⅓ cup cornmeal
1 teaspoon baking powder
¼ cup milk
1 tablespoon canola oil
⅓ cup shredded Cheddar cheese

1. Add vegetable juice, beans, tomatoes with liquid, zucchini, carrots, water, parsnip, barley, bay leaf, thyme and rosemary to 3-quart saucepan. Bring to a boil over high heat. Reduce heat to medium-low. Cover; simmer 20 to 25 minutes or until tender, stirring occasionally. Remove and discard bay leaf.

2. Combine flour, cornmeal and baking powder in small bowl. Combine milk and oil in separate small bowl; stir into flour mixture. Stir in cheese. Drop dough by spoonfuls to make 4 mounds onto boiling stew. Cover; simmer 10 to 12 minutes or until toothpick inserted near center of dumpling comes out clean.

Makes 4 servings

Hearty Minestrone Soup

2 cans (10¾ ounces each) condensed Italian tomato soup
3 cups water
3 cups cooked vegetables, such as zucchini, peas, corn or beans
2 cups cooked ditalini pasta
1⅓ cups *French's®* *Taste Toppers™* French Fried Onions

Combine soup and water in large saucepan. Add vegetables and pasta. Bring to a boil. Reduce heat. Cook until heated through, stirring often.

Place *Taste Toppers* in microwavable dish. Microwave on HIGH 1 minute or until *Taste Toppers* are golden.

Ladle soup into individual bowls. Sprinkle with *Taste Toppers*.   *Makes 6 servings*

Prep Time: 10 minutes
Cook Time: 5 minutes

Kansas City Steak Soup

Nonstick cooking spray
½ pound ground sirloin or ground round beef
1 cup chopped onion
3 cups frozen mixed vegetables
2 cups water
1 can (14½ ounces) stewed tomatoes, undrained
1 cup sliced celery
1 beef bouillon cube
¾ teaspoon black pepper
1 can (10½ ounces) defatted beef broth
½ cup all-purpose flour

1. Spray Dutch oven with cooking spray. Heat over medium-high heat until hot. Add beef and onion. Cook and stir 5 minutes or until beef is browned.

2. Add vegetables, water, tomatoes with liquid, celery, bouillon cube, and pepper. Bring to a boil. Whisk together broth and flour until smooth; add to beef mixture, stirring constantly. Return mixture to a boil. Reduce heat to low. Cover and simmer 15 minutes, stirring frequently.   *Makes 6 servings*

Albondigas Soup

1 pound lean ground beef
2 eggs, slightly beaten
¼ cup blue cornmeal or fine
   dry bread crumbs
1 clove garlic, minced
1 tablespoon chopped fresh
   mint *or* 1 teaspoon
   crumbled dried mint
½ teaspoon salt
¼ teaspoon ground cumin
   Dash black pepper
6 cups water
3 cans (10¾ ounces each)
   condensed beef broth
1 small onion, chopped
¼ cup sliced celery
1 carrot, chopped
1 zucchini, chopped
1 yellow crookneck squash,
   chopped
½ bunch spinach, stems
   removed, leaves cut
   into ½-inch slices
   Cilantro sprigs for
   garnish
2 limes, cut into wedges

1. To make meatballs, combine ground beef, eggs, cornmeal, garlic, mint, salt, cumin and pepper. Shape mixture into 1-inch balls; set aside.

2. To make soup, combine water, beef broth, onion and celery in 5-quart saucepan or Dutch oven. Bring to a boil. Reduce heat; simmer, uncovered, 10 minutes.

3. Add meatballs to broth. Cook, uncovered, 5 minutes. Spoon off fat and foam from surface of broth. Add carrot, zucchini and squash; simmer, uncovered, 20 minutes or until vegetables are tender.

4. Add spinach to soup; cook, uncovered, 5 minutes. Serve in individual bowls. Garnish with cilantro. Pass lime wedges at the table to squeeze onto individual servings.   *Makes 6 servings*

All-in-One Burger Stew

1 pound lean ground beef
2 cups frozen Italian
  vegetables
1 can (14½ ounces)
  chopped tomatoes
  with basil and garlic,
  undrained
1 can (about 14 ounces)
  beef broth
2½ cups uncooked medium
  egg noodles
  Salt and black pepper

1. Cook meat in Dutch oven or large skillet over medium-high heat until no longer pink, stirring to separate meat. Drain drippings.

2. Add vegetables, tomatoes with juice and broth; bring to a boil over high heat.

3. Add noodles; reduce heat to medium. Cover and cook 12 to 15 minutes or until noodles have absorbed liquid and vegetables are tender. Add salt and pepper to taste.

Makes 6 servings

Prep & Cook Time: 25 minutes

Basil-Vegetable Soup

1 package (9 ounces)
  frozen cut green beans
1 can (15 ounces)
  cannellini or Great
  Northern beans,
  undrained
3 medium carrots, sliced
3 medium zucchini or
  yellow squash, sliced
2 quarts beef broth
2 cloves garlic, minced
  Salt and black pepper
2 to 3 ounces uncooked
  vermicelli or spaghetti
½ cup tightly packed fresh
  basil leaves, finely
  chopped
  Grated Romano cheese

Combine beans, carrots, zucchini, broth and garlic in Dutch oven. Bring to a boil over high heat. Reduce heat to low. Cover; simmer until carrots are tender. Season with salt and pepper. Add vermicelli; bring to a boil over high heat. Reduce heat to low. Simmer until pasta is tender, yet firm. (Pasta may be cooked separately; add to soup just before serving.) Add basil; simmer until tender. Serve with cheese.

Makes 10 to 12 servings

Cheesy Broccoli Soup

....

¼ cup chopped onion
1 tablespoon butter or
    margarine
1½ cups milk
¾ pound (12 ounces)
    VELVEETA®
    Pasteurized Prepared
    Cheese Product, cut up
1 package (10 ounces)
    frozen chopped
    broccoli, thawed,
    drained
Dash pepper

1. Cook and stir onion in butter in large saucepan on medium-high heat until tender.

2. Add remaining ingredients; stir on low heat until Velveeta is melted and soup is thoroughly heated.

Makes 4 (¾-cup) servings

Prep Time: 10 minutes
Cook Time: 15 minutes

Chunky Vegetarian Chili

....

1 tablespoon vegetable oil
1 medium green bell
    pepper, chopped
1 medium onion, chopped
3 cloves garlic, minced
2 cans (14½ ounces each)
    Mexican-style
    tomatoes, undrained
1 can (15 ounces) kidney
    beans, rinsed, drained
1 can (15 ounces) pinto
    beans, rinsed, drained
1 can (11 ounces) whole-
    kernel corn, drained
2½ cups water
1 cup uncooked rice
2 tablespoons chili powder
1½ teaspoons ground cumin
Sour cream (optional)

Heat oil in 3-quart saucepan or Dutch oven over medium-high heat. Add bell pepper, onion and garlic and cook and stir 5 minutes or until tender. Add tomatoes, beans, corn, water, rice, chili powder and cumin; stir well. Bring to a boil. Reduce heat; cover. Simmer 30 minutes, stirring occasionally. To serve, top with sour cream, if desired.

Makes 6 servings

Favorite recipe from USA Rice Federation

Cheesy Broccoli Soup

White Bean and Escarole Soup

1½ cups dried baby lima
   beans
1 teaspoon olive oil
½ cup chopped celery
⅓ cup coarsely chopped
   onion
2 cloves garlic, minced
2 cans (10 ounces each)
   no-salt-added whole
   tomatoes, undrained,
   chopped
½ cup chopped fresh parsley
2 tablespoons fresh
   rosemary
¼ teaspoon black pepper
3 cups shredded fresh
   escarole

1. Place dried lima beans in large glass bowl; cover completely with water. Soak 6 to 8 hours or overnight. Drain beans; place in large saucepan or Dutch oven. Cover beans with about 3 cups water; bring to a boil over high heat. Reduce heat to low. Cover and simmer about 1 hour or until soft. Drain; set aside.

2. Heat oil in small skillet over medium heat. Add celery, onion and garlic; cook until onion is tender. Remove from heat.

3. Add celery mixture and tomatoes with liquid to beans. Stir in parsley, rosemary and black pepper. Cover and simmer over low heat 15 minutes. Add escarole; simmer 5 minutes.

Makes 6 (1½-cup) servings

Hearty Meatless Chili

1 envelope LIPTON®
RECIPE SECRETS®
Onion or Onion-
Mushroom Soup Mix
4 cups water
1 can (16 ounces) chick-
peas or garbanzo beans,
rinsed and drained
1 can (16 ounces) red
kidney beans, rinsed
and drained
1 can (14½ ounces) whole
peeled tomatoes,
undrained and
chopped
1 cup lentils, rinsed and
drained
1 large rib celery, coarsely
chopped
1 tablespoon chili powder
2 teaspoons ground cumin
(optional)
1 medium clove garlic,
finely chopped

In 4-quart saucepan or stockpot,
combine all ingredients. Bring
to a boil over high heat. Reduce
heat to low and simmer covered,
stirring occasionally, 20 minutes
or until lentils are almost tender.

Remove cover and simmer,
stirring occasionally, an
additional 20 minutes or until
liquid is almost absorbed and
lentils are tender.
Makes about 4 (2-cup) servings

Note: For spicier chili, add
¼ teaspoon crushed red pepper
flakes.

Serving Suggestion: Serve over
hot cooked brown or white rice
and top with shredded Cheddar
cheese.

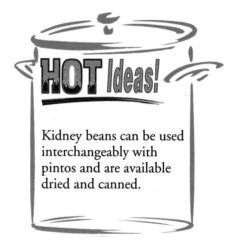

Kidney beans can be used
interchangeably with
pintos and are available
dried and canned.

Greek Salad

8 leaves romaine lettuce
2 tomatoes, cut into eighths
1 medium red onion, sliced
   or 3 green onions,
   chopped
½ cucumber, sliced
2 ounces feta cheese,
   crumbled
3 tablespoons chopped
   fresh parsley
8 oil-cured black olives
4 anchovies (optional)
French Salad Dressing
   (recipe follows)

Slice lettuce with knife into
⅛-inch-wide strips. In medium
bowl, combine lettuce, tomatoes,
onion, cucumber, cheese, parsley,
olives and anchovies, if desired.
Serve with French Salad
Dressing.

Makes 4 to 6 servings

French Salad Dressing

1 clove garlic, crushed
½ teaspoon salt
¼ teaspoon dry mustard
¼ teaspoon freshly ground
   black pepper
¼ teaspoon dried salad
   seasoning
¼ cup FILIPPO BERIO®
   Olive Oil
¼ cup white wine vinegar*
   or lemon juice, divided

*Dressing may be varied by using
tarragon vinegar.

In small bowl, combine garlic,
salt, mustard, pepper and salad
seasoning. Whisk in olive oil
and vinegar until thoroughly
mixed. Store dressing, in tightly
covered container, in refrigerator
up to 1 week. Shake well before
using.   *Makes about ½ cup*

Greek Salad

Garden Vegetable Linguine

8 ounces uncooked linguine
1 pound HILLSHIRE FARM® Smoked Sausage, sliced
5 green or red bell peppers, cut into strips
4 to 5 carrots, sliced
1 package (10 ounces) frozen peas
¾ cup pitted black olives
1 cup Italian salad dressing
Pinch garlic powder
Pinch dried oregano leaves

Cook linguine according to package directions; drain and keep warm. Sauté Smoked Sausage with peppers, carrots, peas and olives in large skillet over medium-high heat. Combine salad dressing, linguine and sausage mixture in large serving bowl. Toss with garlic powder and oregano. Serve hot or cold.

Makes 6 servings

Easy Chef's Salad

1 package (16 ounces) DOLE® Classic Salad (8 cups)
1½ cups DOLE® Broccoli Florets
1 large tomato, cut into thin wedges
4 ounces deli-sliced smoked turkey or chicken, cut into ½-inch strips
¾ cup cubed low fat Cheddar, Monterey Jack or mozzarella cheese
¼ cup feta or goat cheese
¾ cup fat free or light ranch salad dressing

• Toss together salad, broccoli, tomato, turkey and cheeses in large serving bowl.

• Pour dressing over salad; toss to evenly coat.

Makes 4 servings

Prep Time: 15 minutes

CONTENTS

QUICK & EASY CASSEROLES

Carolina Baked Beans & Pork Chops

Prep Time: 10 minutes   Cook Time: 30 minutes

- **2 cans (16 ounces *each*) pork and beans**
- **½ cup *each* chopped onion and green bell pepper**
- **¼ cup FRENCH'S® CLASSIC YELLOW® Mustard**
- **¼ cup packed light brown sugar**
- **2 tablespoons FRENCH'S® Worcestershire Sauce**
- **1 tablespoon FRANK'S® REDHOT® Sauce**
- **6 boneless pork chops (1 inch thick)**

1. Preheat oven to 400°F. Combine all ingredients *except pork chops* in 3-quart shallow baking dish; mix well. Arrange chops on top, turning once to coat with sauce.

2. Bake, uncovered, 30 to 35 minutes or until pork is no longer pink in center. Stir beans around chops once during baking. Serve with green beans or mashed potatoes, if desired.

Makes 6 servings

Carolina Baked Beans & Pork Chop

Sweet 'n' Sour Country Ribs

Prep Time: 10 minutes   Cook Time: about 1 hour

- 3 **pounds country-style pork ribs, fat trimmed**
- 3 **large sweet potatoes, peeled and cut into 2-inch chunks**
- 2 **cups apple juice**
- ¼ **cup cider vinegar**
- ¼ **cup FRENCH'S® Worcestershire Sauce**
- ¼ **cup packed brown sugar**
- 2 **tablespoons FRENCH'S® Hearty Deli Brown Mustard**
- 2 **tart green apples, cored and cut into 1-inch chunks**
- 1 **tablespoon cornstarch**

1. Heat *1 tablespoon oil* in 6-quart saucepot or Dutch oven over high heat. Cook ribs 10 minutes or until well-browned on all sides; drain fat.

2. Add potatoes to ribs. Whisk together apple juice, vinegar, Worcestershire, sugar and mustard. Pour over rib mixture; stir well. Heat to boiling. Reduce heat to low. Cook, covered, 40 minutes or until pork is tender and no longer pink in center, stirring occasionally.

3. Stir in apples; cook 5 minutes or until tender. Transfer ribs, potatoes and apples to platter; keep warm. Combine cornstarch with *2 tablespoons water*. Stir into pot. Heat to boiling, whisking constantly. Cook 1 to 2 minutes or until liquid thickens, stirring often. Serve with corn and crusty bread, if desired.

Makes 6 servings (with 2 cups gravy)

20 Minute Marinade: Marinate 1 pound steak, chicken or chops for 20 minutes in ¼ cup FRENCH'S Worcestershire Sauce.

Mexican Chicken Bake

Prep Time: 10 minutes   Cook Time: 35 minutes

    1 pound boneless skinless chicken thighs, cut into strips
    2 cans (8 ounces *each*) tomato sauce
    1 can (11 ounces) Mexican-style corn kernels, drained
1⅓ cups FRENCH'S® Taste Toppers™ French Fried Onions,
        divided
    2 tablespoons FRANK'S® REDHOT® Sauce
    ½ teaspoon dried oregano leaves
    ½ teaspoon ground cumin
    ¼ teaspoon garlic powder

1. Preheat oven to 350°F. Combine chicken, tomato sauce, corn, ⅔ *cup* Taste Toppers, REDHOT Sauce and seasonings in lightly greased 2-quart baking dish. Stir until chicken is well coated.

2. Bake, uncovered, 30 minutes or until chicken is no longer pink and sauce is hot. Stir. Top with remaining ⅔ *cup* onions. Bake 5 minutes or until onions are golden. Serve with hot cooked rice, if desired.   *Makes 4 servings*

Pork Chop & Wild Rice Bake

Prep Time: 5 minutes   Cook Time: 35 minutes

    1 package (6 ounces) seasoned long grain & wild rice mix
1⅓ cups FRENCH'S® Taste Toppers™ French Fried Onions,
        divided
    1 package (10 ounces) frozen cut green beans,
        thawed and drained
    ¼ cup orange juice
    1 teaspoon grated orange peel
    4 boneless pork chops (1 inch thick)

1. Preheat oven to 375°F. Combine rice mix and seasoning packet, *2 cups water*, ⅔ *cup* Taste Toppers, green beans, orange juice and orange peel in 2-quart shallow baking dish. Arrange pork chops on top.

2. Bake, uncovered, 30 minutes or until pork chops are no longer pink near center. Sprinkle chops with remaining ⅔ *cup* onions. Bake 5 minutes or until onions are golden.   *Makes 4 servings*

Jamaican Meat Patties

Prep Time: 15 minutes   Cook Time: 25 minutes

1 **pound ground beef**
1 **onion, chopped**
1 **clove garlic, minced**
¼ **cup FRANK'S® REDHOT® Sauce**
2¼ **teaspoons curry powder, divided**
1 **teaspoon dried thyme leaves**
1 **egg, beaten**
2 **sheets folded refrigerated unbaked pie crusts (15 ounce package)**

1. Cook beef, onion and garlic in nonstick skillet 5 minutes or until meat is browned, stirring to separate meat. Drain fat. Stir in REDHOT Sauce, *½ cup water, 2 teaspoons* curry powder and thyme. Cook 5 minutes or until liquid is evaporated, stirring often. Cool slightly. Mix egg with *1 tablespoon water* and remaining *¼ teaspoon* curry powder; set aside.

2. Preheat oven to 400°F. Roll out each pie crust sheet into slightly larger round on lightly floured board. Cut out 10 rounds using 5-inch cookie cutter, re-rolling scraps as necessary. Brush edge of rounds with some of egg mixture. Spoon about 3 tablespoons cooled meat mixture in center of each round. Fold rounds in half, pressing edges with floured fork to seal.

3. Place patties onto lightly greased baking sheets. Brush tops with remaining egg mixture. Bake 15 minutes or until crusts are crisp. *Makes 10 patties*

Tip

A small bowl measuring 5-inches across may be used for the cookie cutter. Patties can be prepared ahead and frozen before baking; wrap securely. Bake, uncovered, at 400°F for 15 minutes. To make party-size appetizers, use a 3-inch round cutter.

Crispy Onion Chicken

Prep Time: 10 minutes   Cook Time: 20 minutes

**1⅓ cups FRENCH'S® Taste Toppers™ French Fried Onions
2 to 3 tablespoons FRENCH'S® Mustard (any flavor)
4 to 6 boneless skinless chicken breast halves**

1. Preheat oven to 350°F. Place Taste Toppers in plastic bag. Press with rolling pin until onions are lightly crushed. Transfer to sheet of waxed paper.

2. Spread mustard evenly on chicken. Coat with onion crumbs; pressing gently to adhere.

3. Place in baking pan. Bake 20 minutes or until chicken is no longer pink in center.   *Makes 4 to 6 servings*

Stuffed Green Pepper Casserole

Prep Time: 5 minutes   Cook Time: 20 minutes

**1 pound ground beef
1 jar (28 ounces) spaghetti sauce
¼ cup FRENCH'S® Worcestershire Sauce
1¼ cups uncooked instant rice
3 large green bell peppers
1 cup (4 ounces) shredded Cheddar cheese**

1. Cook beef in nonstick skillet 5 minutes or until meat is browned, stirring to separate meat. Drain fat. Stir in spaghetti sauce and Worcestershire. Heat to boiling. Stir in rice. Remove from heat. Cover; let stand 10 minutes.

2. Halve peppers lengthwise; remove seeds and ribs. Cut into 1½-inch squares. Place into 2-quart microwave-safe baking dish with *¼ cup water*. Cover. Microwave on HIGH 5 minutes or until crisp-tender, stirring twice; drain water. Spoon ground beef mixture over peppers. Sprinkle with cheese.

3. Microwave 1 to 2 minutes or until cheese is melted.
                                   Makes 6 servings

Crispy Onion Chicken

Oniony BBQ Meatloaf

Prep Time: 10 minutes   Cook Time: about 1 hour

- **2 pounds ground beef**
- **1⅓ cups FRENCH'S® Taste Toppers™ French Fried Onions, divided**
- **1 cup barbecue sauce, divided**
- **½ cup dry seasoned bread crumbs**
- **2 eggs**
- **¼ cup FRENCH'S® Worcestershire Sauce**

1. Preheat oven to 350°F. Combine beef, ⅔ *cup* Taste Toppers, ½ *cup* barbecue sauce, bread crumbs, eggs and Worcestershire in large bowl; stir with fork until well blended.

2. Place meat mixture into greased 2-quart shallow baking dish; shape into 9×5-inch loaf. Bake 1 hour or until no longer pink; drain. Pour remaining ½ *cup* sauce over meat loaf and top with remaining ⅔ *cup* onions. Bake 5 minutes or until onions are golden.

3. Cut into slices. Serve with deli coleslaw and rolls, if desired.

Makes 6 to 8 servings

Tip

For a change of pace use ketchup, tomato sauce or marinara sauce for the barbecue sauce.

Enchiladas

Prep Time: 10 minutes   Cook Time: 35 minutes

  1 **package (10 ounces) fully cooked carved chicken breast***
  1 **cup cooked rice**
  2 **jars (12 ounces *each*) salsa, divided**
  1 **can (15 to 19 ounces) black beans, rinsed and drained**
1⅓ **cups FRENCH'S® Taste Toppers™ French Fried Onions, divided**
  1 **cup (4 ounces) shredded Cheddar cheese, divided**
12 **(8-inch) flour tortillas**

You may substitute 2 cups shredded cooked chicken.

1. Preheat oven to 350°F. Combine chicken, rice, *1 cup* salsa, beans, ⅔ *cup* Taste Toppers and ½ *cup* cheese in large bowl. Spread about ½ cup mixture down center of each tortilla. Roll up tortillas enclosing filling. Place seam-side down in greased 15×10-inch baking pan.

2. Pour remaining salsa on top of tortillas. Cover dish. Bake 30 minutes or until heated through.

3. Top with remaining ½ *cup* cheese and ⅔ *cup* onions. Bake 5 minutes or until onions are golden.   *Makes 6 servings*

Zesty Citrus Chicken

Prep Time: 5 minutes   Cook Time: about 1 hour

  1 **(3- to 4-pound) chicken, cut into eighths**
½ **cup teriyaki baste and glaze sauce**
⅓ **cup FRANK'S® REDHOT® Sauce**
⅓ **cup FRENCH'S® Hearty Deli Brown Mustard**
¼ **cup lemon *or* lime juice**
  1 **tablespoon grated peeled ginger**

1. Preheat oven to 400°F. Place chicken into greased 3-quart baking dish. Bake 30 minutes; drain fat.

2. Combine remaining ingredients. Pour over chicken pieces. Bake 25 to 30 minutes or until chicken is no longer pink near bone; basting occasionally. Serve warm with pan juices. Serve with hot cooked rice or steamed vegetables, if desired.

Makes 6 servings

Green Bean & Turkey Bake

Prep Time: 10 minutes   Cook Time: 50 minutes

    1 can (10¾ ounces) condensed cream of mushroom soup
    ¾ cup milk
    2 packages (9 ounces *each*) frozen cut green beans,
        thawed
    2 cups (12 ounces) cubed cooked turkey *or* chicken
    1⅓ cups FRENCH'S® Taste Toppers™ French Fried Onions,
        divided
    1½ cups (6 ounces) shredded Cheddar cheese, divided
    3 cups hot mashed potatoes

1. Preheat oven to 375°F. In 3-quart casserole, combine soup, milk and ⅛ *teaspoon pepper;* mix well. Stir in beans, turkey, ⅔ *cup* Taste Toppers and *1 cup* cheese. Spoon mashed potatoes on top.

2. Bake, uncovered, 45 minutes or until hot. Sprinkle with remaining ½ *cup* cheese and ⅔ *cup* onions. Bake 3 minutes or until onions are golden.   *Makes 6 servings*

Microwave Directions: Prepare mixture as above *except do not* top with potatoes. Cover casserole with vented plastic wrap. Microwave on HIGH 15 minutes or until heated through, stirring halfway. Uncover. Top with mashed potatoes, remaining cheese and onions. Microwave on HIGH 2 to 4 minutes. Let stand 5 minutes.

Tip

Two (14½-ounce) cans cut green beans (drained) may be used instead of frozen beans. You may substitute instant mashed potatoes prepared according to package directions for 6 servings.

Chicken Dijon & Pasta

Prep Time: 15 minutes   Cook Time: about 1 hour

1 (3- to 4-pound) chicken, cut-up and skinned, if desired
⅓ cup FRENCH'S® Dijon Mustard
⅓ cup Italian salad dressing
1 can (10¾ ounces) condensed cream of chicken soup
4 cups hot cooked rotini pasta (8 ounces uncooked)
1⅓ cups FRENCH'S® Taste Toppers™ French Fried Onions, divided
1 cup diced tomatoes
1 cup diced zucchini
2 tablespoons minced parsley *or* basil leaves (optional)

1. Preheat oven to 400°F. Place chicken in shallow roasting pan. Mix mustard and dressing. Spoon half of mixture over chicken. Bake, uncovered, 40 minutes.

2. Combine soup, *½ cup water* and remaining mustard mixture. Toss pasta with sauce, *⅔ cup* Taste Toppers, vegetables and parsley. Spoon mixture around chicken.

3. Bake, uncovered, 15 minutes or until chicken is no longer pink in center. Sprinkle with remaining *⅔ cup* onions. Bake 1 minute or until onions are golden.   *Makes 6 servings*

Confetti Pineapple Baked Ham Steak

Prep Time: 5 minutes   Cook Time: 20 minutes

1 pound ready-to-serve ham steak
1 can (8 ounces) crushed pineapple, drained
1 cup diced red *or* green bell peppers
3 tablespoons FRENCH'S® Honey Mustard
2 tablespoons lightly packed brown sugar
1/16 teaspoon ground cloves

1. Preheat oven to 425°F. Score edge of ham steak. Place in 2-quart baking dish. Combine remaining ingredients in small bowl. Spoon pineapple mixture on top of ham steak.

2. Bake, uncovered, 20 minutes or until hot and bubbly. Serve with hot cooked rice, if desired.   *Makes 4 servings*

Chicken Dijon & Pasta

94

Buffalo Baked Chicken

Prep Time: 5 minutes   Cook Time: 1 hour

**4 pounds chicken wings and thighs (or cut-up chicken
    pieces)**
¾ cup FRANK'S® REDHOT® Sauce, divided
¼ cup butter *or* margarine, melted

1. Preheat oven to 425°F. Arrange chicken in greased baking pan.
Brush chicken pieces with ¼ *cup* REDHOT Sauce. Bake 1 hour or
until no longer pink in center; drain.

2. Combine remaining ½ *cup* REDHOT Sauce and butter in large
bowl. Dip chicken pieces into sauce mixture to coat. Serve with
cooked rice and salad tossed with blue cheese dressing, if
desired.   *Makes 6 servings*

Chicken Tetrazzini

Prep Time: 5 minutes   Cook Time: 35 minutes

1 can (10¾ ounces) condensed cream of mushroom soup
**1⅓ cups FRENCH'S® Taste Toppers™ French Fried Onions,
    divided**
1¼ cups milk
1 cup (4 ounces) shredded Monterey Jack cheese, divided
2 tablespoons minced parsley
¼ teaspoon dried oregano leaves
¼ teaspoon garlic powder
4 cups cooked spaghetti (8 ounces uncooked)
2 cups (10 ounces) finely cubed cooked chicken
1 package (10 ounces) frozen peas and carrots, thawed

1. Preheat oven to 350°F. In large bowl, combine soup, ⅔ *cup*
Taste Toppers, milk, ½ *cup* cheese, parsley, oregano and garlic
powder. Stir in spaghetti, chicken and vegetables. Pour into
lightly greased 2-quart baking dish.

2. Bake, uncovered, 30 minutes or until heated through. Stir. Top
with remaining ⅔ *cup* onions and ½ *cup* cheese. Bake 5 minutes
or until onions are golden.   *Makes 6 servings*

Buffalo Baked Chicken

Saucy Turkey & Pasta

Prep Time: 10 minutes   Cook Time: 45 minutes

    8 ounces uncooked fusilli or linguine pasta, broken in half
 1⅓ cups FRENCH'S® Taste Toppers™ French Fried Onions, divided
    2 cups (12 ounces) cubed cooked turkey *or* chicken
    1 can (10¾ ounces) condensed cream of chicken soup
    1 jar (8 ounces) picante sauce
   ½ cup sour cream
    1 cup (4 ounces) shredded Cheddar cheese

1. Preheat oven to 350°F. Cook pasta according to package directions using shortest cooking time; drain. Layer pasta, ⅔ cup Taste Toppers and turkey in greased 2-quart shallow baking dish.

2. Combine soup, picante sauce and sour cream. Pour over turkey. Cover; bake 40 minutes or until heated through, stirring halfway during cooking. Sprinkle with cheese and remaining ⅔ cup onions. Bake 5 minutes or until onions are golden.

Makes 4 to 6 servings

Santa Fe Chicken & Pasta

Prep Time: 10 minutes   Cook Time: 43 minutes

    1 jar (12 ounces) mild chunky salsa
    1 can (10¾ ounces) condensed Cheddar cheese soup
   ¾ cup sour cream
    5 cups hot cooked ziti pasta (8 ounces uncooked)
 1⅓ cups FRENCH'S® Taste Toppers™ French Fried Onions, divided
    1 package (10 ounces) fully cooked carved chicken breast (2 cups cut-up chicken)
    1 cup (4 ounces) cubed Monterey Jack cheese with jalapeño

1. Preheat oven to 375°F. In large bowl, mix salsa, soup and sour cream. Stir in pasta, ⅔ cup Taste Toppers, chicken and cheese; mix well. Spoon into 3-quart casserole.

2. Cover; bake 40 minutes or until hot and bubbly. Stir.

3. Sprinkle with remaining ⅔ cup onions. Bake 3 minutes or until onions are golden.

Makes 8 servings

Crunchy Onion Coated Steak 'n' Tomatoes

Prep Time: 10 minutes   Cook Time: 35 minutes

1⅓ cups FRENCH'S® Taste Toppers™ French Fried Onions
½ cup seasoned dry bread crumbs
2 tablespoons chopped fresh parsley
¾ teaspoon garlic powder
2 pounds boneless sirloin steak, fat trimmed (1 inch thick)
4 large ripe tomatoes, cut in half crosswise
4 tablespoons FRENCH'S® Dijon Mustard

1. Preheat oven to 350°F. Lightly crush Taste Toppers with back of spoon in medium bowl. Stir in bread crumbs, parsley and garlic powder; mix well.

2. Place steak in large roasting pan. Arrange tomatoes, cut-side up around steak. Spread *3 tablespoons* mustard on top and sides of steak. Brush remaining mustard on top of tomatoes. Sprinkle tomatoes with *½ cup* onion mixture. Press remaining mixture firmly on steak.

3. Bake, uncovered, 35 to 40 minutes or until steak is medium-rare (or to desired doneness) and tomatoes are tender. Let meat rest 10 minutes before slicing. Serve with extra FRENCH'S Dijon Mustard.   *Makes 8 servings*

Kid's Choice Meatballs

Prep Time: 10 minutes   Cook Time: 20 minutes

- 1½ **pounds ground beef**
- ¼ **cup dry seasoned bread crumbs**
- ¼ **cup grated Parmesan cheese**
- 3 **tablespoons FRENCH'S® Worcestershire Sauce**
- 1 **egg**
- 2 **jars (14 ounces *each*) spaghetti sauce**

1. Preheat oven to 425°F. In bowl, gently mix beef, bread crumbs, cheese, Worcestershire and egg. Shape into 1-inch meatballs. Place on rack in roasting pan. Bake 15 minutes or until cooked.

2. In large saucepan, combine meatballs and spaghetti sauce. Cook until heated through. Serve over cooked pasta.

Makes 6 to 8 servings (about 48 meatballs)

Quick Meatball Tip: On waxed paper, pat meat mixture into 8×6×1-inch rectangle. With knife, cut crosswise and lengthwise into 1-inch rows. Roll each small square into a ball.

Caribbean Chicken

Prep Time: 40 minutes   Cook Time: 45 minutes

- 2 **pounds boneless skinless chicken thighs**
- ½ **cup FRANK'S® REDHOT® Sauce**
- 2 **tablespoons FRENCH'S® Worcestershire Sauce**
- 1 **green onion, minced**
- 1 **clove garlic, minced**
- 1 **teaspoon dried thyme leaves**
- 1 **teaspoon ground allspice**
- ¼ **teaspoon *each* ground cinnamon and ground nutmeg**

1. Place chicken into lightly greased large roasting pan. Combine remaining ingredients in small bowl. Pour marinade over chicken, turning to coat evenly. Cover pan; marinate in refrigerator 30 minutes or overnight.

2. Preheat oven to 350°F. Bake chicken, uncovered, 45 minutes or until no longer pink in center, basting occasionally. Serve with hot cooked rice, if desired.

Makes 6 to 8 servings

Kid's Choice Meatballs

SPEEDY SKILLET SUPPERS

Savory Skillet Lemon Chicken

Prep Time: 5 minutes   Cook Time: 15 minutes

- **4 boneless skinless chicken breast halves**
- **1 cup chicken broth**
- **1⅓ cups FRENCH'S® Taste Toppers™ French Fried Onions, divided**
- **1 tablespoon lemon juice**
- **4 thin slices lemon**

1. Sprinkle chicken with salt and black pepper to taste. Coat chicken in *¼ cup flour* on sheet of waxed paper; shake off excess. Heat *1 tablespoon oil* in large nonstick skillet until hot. Cook chicken 10 minutes or until thoroughly browned on both sides.

2. Stir in chicken broth, *⅔ cup* Taste Toppers, lemon juice and lemon slices. Heat to boiling. Reduce heat to medium-low. Cook, covered, 5 minutes or until chicken is no longer pink in center and sauce thickens slightly, stirring occasionally. Sprinkle with remaining *⅔ cup* onions. Serve with hot cooked rice, if desired.

Makes 4 servings

Savory Skillet Lemon Chicken

Buffalo-Style Skillet Steak

Prep Time: 20 minutes   Cook Time: 12 minutes

1¼ **pounds boneless sirloin steak (1 inch thick)**
4 **tablespoons FRANK'S® REDHOT® Sauce, divided**
Garlic powder *and* celery salt to taste
½ **pound sliced fresh mushrooms**
2 **tablespoons crumbled blue cheese**

1. Cut steak crosswise into 4 servings. Brush each lightly with *1 tablespoon* REDHOT Sauce on both sides. Sprinkle with garlic powder and celery salt. Cover; let stand in refrigerator 15 minutes or longer, if desired.

2. Melt *1 tablespoon butter or margarine* in large skillet over medium-high heat. Add mushrooms and cook, stirring, until browned. Divide among 4 dinner plates; keep warm.

3. In same skillet, melt *1 tablespoon butter or margarine* over high heat. Cook steaks 1 minute per side. Reduce heat to medium and cook 3 minutes per side for medium-rare, or to desired doneness. Pour remaining *3 tablespoons* REDHOT Sauce over steaks; turn to coat. Sprinkle with blue cheese. Serve on top of mushrooms. Pour any pan juices on top.   *Makes 4 servings*

Easy Chicken & Vegetable Stir-Fry

Prep Time: 5 minutes   Cook Time: 10 minutes

1½ **pounds boneless skinless chicken, cut into strips**
1 **package (21 ounces) teriyaki stir-fry frozen vegetable combination***
1⅓ **cups FRENCH'S® Taste Toppers™ French Fried Onions**

*Or use 4 cups frozen vegetables and ¾ cup teriyaki stir-fry sauce.

1. Heat *1 tablespoon oil* in large nonstick skillet until hot. Stir-fry chicken until browned.

2. Add vegetables and contents of sauce packet. Stir-fry until crisp-tender.

3. Microwave Taste Toppers 1 minute on HIGH. Sprinkle over stir-fry. Serve with hot cooked rice, if desired.

Makes 6 servings

Buffalo-Style Skillet Steak

Southwestern Skillet Macaroni

Prep Time: 10 minutes   Cook Time: 10 minutes

1½ cups elbow macaroni
1 pound ground beef
¼ cup chili powder
1 can (28 ounces) crushed tomatoes in purée
⅓ cup FRANK'S® REDHOT® Sauce
1 cup (4 ounces) shredded Cheddar cheese

1. Cook macaroni in boiling water 5 minutes. Drain.

2. In large nonstick skillet, cook ground beef with chili powder until meat is browned. Add tomatoes and REDHOT Sauce. Heat to boiling. Reduce heat to medium. Cook 5 minutes.

3. Add macaroni; cook 5 minutes or until pasta is tender and has absorbed excess liquid. Sprinkle with cheese.

Makes 4 servings

Mediterranean Chicken

Prep Time: 10 minutes   Cook Time: 30 minutes

1 (3- to 4-pound) chicken, cut-up and skinned
1 can (28 ounces) crushed tomatoes in purée
1 onion, thinly sliced
1 can (2¼ ounces) sliced black olives, drained (½ cup)
3 tablespoons FRENCH'S® Worcestershire Sauce
2 tablespoons capers
3 cloves garlic, minced
1 teaspoon dried oregano leaves

1. Place chicken in plastic bag. Add *¼ cup flour;* shake to coat. Heat *1 tablespoon oil* in large nonstick skillet over high heat. Cook chicken 10 minutes or until browned on both sides. Drain.

2. Stir in remaining ingredients. Heat to boiling. Reduce heat to medium-low. Cook, covered, 20 minutes or until chicken is no longer pink in center. Serve over hot cooked couscous or rice, if desired.

Makes 4 servings

Saucy Chicken & Vegetables

Prep Time: 10 minutes   Cook Time: 20 minutes

6 boneless skinless chicken breast halves
1 can (10¾ ounces) condensed cream of chicken soup
**1⅓ cups FRENCH'S® Taste Toppers™ French Fried Onions,
     divided**
1 cup milk *or* water
½ cup grated Parmesan cheese
3 cups bite-size vegetables*
2 teaspoons dried basil leaves

*Try these variations—3 cups cut-up tomatoes, zucchini and asparagus; 3 cups cut-up broccoli and carrots; 1 (16-ounce) package frozen vegetable combination, thawed.

1. Heat *1 tablespoon oil* in 12-inch nonstick skillet until hot. Cook chicken 10 minutes or until thoroughly browned on both sides. Remove; set aside.

2. In same skillet, combine soup, ⅔ *cup* Taste Toppers, milk and cheese. Heat to boiling. Stir in vegetables and basil. Return chicken to skillet. Reduce heat to medium-low. Cook 5 minutes or until chicken is no longer pink in center, stirring occasionally.

3. Top with remaining ⅔ *cup* onions. Serve with hot cooked rice or pasta, if desired.   *Makes 6 servings*

For a crispier onion topping, microwave FRENCH'S Taste Toppers French Fried Onions 1 minute on HIGH.

Honey Mustard BBQ Chicken Stir-Fry

Prep Time: 10 minutes   Cook Time: 15 minutes

1 box (10 ounces) couscous pasta
1 pound boneless chicken, cut into strips
1 medium red bell pepper, cut into thin strips
1 medium onion, sliced
⅓ cup FRENCH'S® Honey Mustard
⅓ cup barbecue sauce

1. Prepare couscous according to package directions. Keep warm.

2. Heat *1 tablespoon oil* in large nonstick skillet over medium-high heat. Stir-fry chicken in batches 5 to 10 minutes or until browned. Transfer to bowl. Drain fat.

3. Heat *1 tablespoon oil* in same skillet until hot. Stir-fry vegetables 3 minutes or until crisp-tender. Return chicken to skillet. Stir in ⅔ *cup water,* mustard and barbecue sauce. Heat to boiling, stirring often. Serve over couscous.

Makes 4 servings

Cheesy Skillet Lasagna

Prep Time: 10 minutes   Cook Time: 10 minutes

1 pound ground beef
2 jars (14 ounces *each*) marinara sauce
2 cups cooked rotini pasta
1⅓ cups FRENCH'S® Taste Toppers™ French Fried Onions, divided
1 cup ricotta cheese
1 cup (4 ounces) shredded mozzarella cheese

1. Cook beef in large skillet until browned; drain. Stir in sauce, pasta and ⅔ *cup* Taste Toppers. Heat to boiling, stirring.

2. Spoon ricotta cheese over beef mixture. Sprinkle with mozzarella cheese and remaining ⅔ *cup* onions. Cover; cook over medium-low heat 3 minutes or until cheese melts.

Makes 4 servings

Honey Mustard BBQ Chicken Stir-Fry

Stir-Fried Pasta with Chicken 'n' Vegetables

Prep Time: 5 minutes   Cook Time: 15 minutes

6 ounces angel hair pasta, broken in thirds (about 3 cups)
¼ cup FRANK'S® REDHOT® Sauce
3 tablespoons soy sauce
2 teaspoons cornstarch
1 tablespoon sugar
½ teaspoon garlic powder
1 pound boneless skinless chicken, cut in ¾-inch cubes
1 package (16 ounces) frozen stir-fry vegetables

1. Cook pasta in boiling water until just tender. Drain. Combine REDHOT Sauce, *¼ cup water*, soy sauce, cornstarch, sugar and garlic powder in small bowl; set aside.

2. Heat *1 tablespoon oil* in large nonstick skillet over high heat. Stir-fry chicken 3 minutes. Add vegetables; stir-fry 3 minutes or until crisp-tender. Add REDHOT Sauce mixture. Heat to boiling. Reduce heat to medium-low. Cook, stirring, 1 to 2 minutes or until sauce is thickened.

3. Stir pasta into skillet; toss to coat evenly. Serve hot.

Makes 4 servings

Bistro Steak au Poivre

Prep Time: 10 minutes   Cook Time: 20 minutes

1½ to 2 pounds boneless sirloin steak (1½ inches thick)
2 cups sliced mushrooms
1 can (10¾ ounces) condensed golden mushroom soup
½ cup dry red wine *or* beef broth
3 tablespoons FRENCH'S® Worcestershire Sauce

1. Rub sides of steak with *¼ teaspoon pepper*. Heat *1 tablespoon oil* over medium-high heat in nonstick skillet. Cook steak about 5 minutes per side for medium-rare or to desired doneness. Transfer steak to platter.

2. Stir-fry mushrooms in same skillet in *1 tablespoon oil* until browned. Stir in soup, wine, Worcestershire and *¼ cup water*. Bring to a boil. Simmer, stirring, 3 minutes. Return steak and juices to skillet. Cook until heated through. Serve with mashed potatoes, if desired.   *Makes 6 servings*

Oniony Chicken Cacciatore

Prep Time: 10 minutes   Cook Time: 25 minutes

2 pounds boneless skinless chicken thighs
2 cups sliced mushrooms
1 red or green bell pepper, thinly sliced
2 cloves garlic, minced
1 jar (28 ounces) marinara sauce
1⅓ cups FRENCH'S® Taste Toppers™ French Fried Onions, divided

1. Heat *1 tablespoon oil* in large nonstick skillet until hot. Cook chicken 5 minutes or until browned on both sides. Remove; set aside.

2. In same skillet, cook and stir mushrooms, pepper and garlic until mushrooms are lightly browned. Stir in sauce and ⅔ cup Taste Toppers. Return chicken to skillet. Heat to boiling. Reduce heat to medium-low. Cook, covered, 15 minutes or until chicken is no longer pink in center, stirring occasionally.

3. Sprinkle chicken with remaining ⅔ cup onions. Serve over pasta, if desired.   *Makes 8 servings*

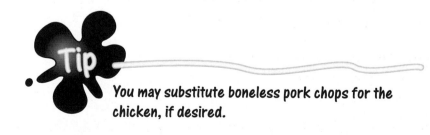

You may substitute boneless pork chops for the chicken, if desired.

Louisiana Red Beans & Rice

Prep Time: 10 minutes   Cook Time: 20 minutes

½ **pound smoked sausage, cut into thin slices (such as
    kielbasa, chorizo or andouille)**
3 **cups cut-up vegetables (onion, bell pepper and celery)**
2 **cloves garlic, minced *or* ½ teaspoon garlic powder**
3 **cans (15 to 19 ounces *each*) red kidney beans, undrained**
¼ **cup FRANK'S® REDHOT® Sauce**
1 **teaspoon dried thyme leaves**
2 **bay leaves**
  Hot cooked rice

1. Cook sausage in large nonstick skillet over medium-high heat
5 minutes or until browned. Add onion, bell pepper, celery and
garlic. Cook and stir 3 minutes or until vegetables are crisp-tender.

2. Stir in beans, REDHOT Sauce and herbs. Heat to boiling.
Reduce heat to medium-low. Cook, uncovered, 10 minutes or
until flavors are blended, stirring occasionally. Discard bay leaves.
Serve over hot cooked rice.   *Makes 6 servings*

Flash in the Pan Chicken & Veggie Stir-Fry

Prep Time: 10 minutes   Cook Time: 10 minutes

1½ **pounds boneless skinless chicken, cut into 1-inch cubes**
 ¼ **cup teriyaki sauce**
 2 **small zucchini, thinly sliced (about ¾ pound)**
 1 **red *or* green bell pepper, cut into strips**
1⅓ **cups FRENCH'S® Taste Toppers™ French Fried Onions,
    divided**
 ½ **cup Italian salad dressing**
 1 **teaspoon cornstarch**

1. Toss chicken with teriyaki sauce. Heat *1 tablespoon oil* in
12-inch nonstick skillet until hot. Stir-fry chicken 5 minutes or until
browned. Add zucchini, pepper and *⅔ cup* Taste Toppers; stir-fry
3 minutes or until vegetables are crisp-tender.

2. Combine dressing with cornstarch; stir into skillet. Heat to
boiling. Cook 2 minutes or until sauce thickens. Sprinkle with
remaining *⅔ cup* onions.   *Makes 6 servings*

Louisiana Red Beans & Rice

Quick 'n' Tangy Beef Stir-Fry

Prep Time: 10 minutes Cook Time: about 10 minutes

SAUCE
- ½ **cup FRENCH'S® Worcestershire Sauce**
- ½ **cup water**
- 2 **tablespoons sugar**
- 2 **teaspoons cornstarch**
- ½ **teaspoon ground ginger**
- ½ **teaspoon garlic powder**

STIR-FRY
- 1 **pound thinly sliced beef steak**
- 3 **cups sliced bell peppers**

1. Combine ingredients for sauce. Marinate beef in ¼ *cup* sauce 5 minutes. Heat *1 tablespoon oil* in large skillet or wok over high heat. Stir-fry beef in batches 5 minutes or until browned.

2. Add peppers; cook 2 minutes. Add remaining sauce; stir-fry until sauce thickens. Serve over hot cooked rice or ramen noodles, if desired.   *Makes 4 servings*

Cheesy Broccoli & Rice with Chicken

Prep Time: 10 minutes   Cook Time: 15 minutes

- 1½ **pounds boneless skinless chicken, cut into strips**
- 1 **package (4.4 ounces) chicken flavor rice & sauce mix**
- 1⅓ **cups FRENCH'S® Taste Toppers™ French Fried Onions, divided**
- 1 **cup *each* chopped broccoli and red bell pepper**
- 1 **cup cubed pasteurized process cheese**

1. Heat *1 tablespoon oil* in large skillet or wok until hot. Stir-fry chicken 5 minutes or until browned. Add rice mix and *2 cups water;* heat to boiling.

2. Stir in ⅔ *cup* Taste Toppers, vegetables and cheese. Simmer, uncovered, 10 minutes or until rice is tender, stirring.

3. Sprinkle remaining ⅔ *cup* onions over rice just before serving.
Makes 6 servings

Quick 'n' Tangy Beef Stir-Fry

Chicken Dijon with Spinach

Prep Time: 15 minutes   Cook Time: about 10 minutes

  1 **pound boneless skinless chicken cutlets**
  2 **cloves garlic, minced**
  ¾ **cup chicken broth**
  ¼ **cup FRENCH'S® Dijon Mustard**
  2 **cups fresh spinach, washed and torn**
  ⅓ **cup heavy cream**
  1 **package (9 ounces) fresh linguine pasta, cooked**

1. Heat *1 tablespoon oil* in large nonstick skillet over high heat. Add chicken; cook 5 minutes or until browned on both sides. Add garlic; cook and stir just until golden.

2. Combine broth and mustard. Pour over chicken. Heat to boiling. Reduce heat to medium-low. Cook 5 minutes or until chicken is no longer pink in center.

3. Stir in spinach and cream. Heat to boiling. Cook 1 minute or until slightly thickened and spinach wilts. Serve over linguine. Garnish with minced parsley, if desired.   *Makes 4 servings*

Glazed Pork Chops & Apples

Prep Time: 10 minutes   Cook Time: 22 minutes

  6 **boneless pork chops (1 inch thick)**
  1 **cup beef broth**
  ¼ **cup cider vinegar**
  ¼ **cup firmly packed brown sugar**
  1⅓ **cups FRENCH'S® Taste Toppers™ French Fried Onions, divided**
  2 **apples, cored and cut into ½-inch wedges**

1. Sprinkle pork chops with salt and black pepper to taste. Coat chops in *¼ cup flour* on sheet of waxed paper; shake off excess. Heat *1 tablespoon oil* in large nonstick skillet until hot. Cook 10 minutes or until thoroughly browned on both sides. Remove; set aside.

2. Stir broth, vinegar, sugar and ⅔ *cup* Taste Toppers into skillet. Heat to boiling, stirring often. Return chops to skillet. Reduce heat to medium-low. Cook, covered, 10 minutes or until pork is no longer pink near bone and sauce thickens slightly, stirring occasionally. Stir in apples; cook 2 minutes.

3. Sprinkle with remaining ⅔ *cup* onions. Serve with rice or mashed potatoes, if desired.   *Makes 6 servings*

Smothered Chicken

Prep Time: 15 minutes   Cook Time: 10 minutes

   6 boneless skinless chicken breast halves, cut into ¾-inch cubes
1½ cups finely chopped vegetables (onion, celery and green bell pepper)
   3 cloves garlic, minced
   1 can (14½ ounces) stewed tomatoes, undrained
   1 can (10¾ ounces) condensed golden mushroom soup
   3 tablespoons FRENCH'S® Worcestershire Sauce

1. Melt *2 tablespoons butter* in large nonstick skillet over medium-high heat. Add chicken; cook and stir 5 minutes or until well browned. Add vegetables and garlic; cook and stir 3 minutes.

2. Stir in tomatoes, soup and Worcestershire. Heat to boiling. Reduce heat to medium-low; cook 2 minutes. Serve with herbed rice, if desired.   *Makes 6 servings*

Tip

One chicken, cut up, may be substituted for the boneless chicken. Brown chicken well in Step 1; drain. Proceed as directed except in Step 2, cook, covered, 30 minutes or until chicken is no longer pink near bone.

Chicken Rustigo

Prep Time: 10 minutes   Cook Time: 21 minutes

4 **boneless skinless chicken breast halves**
1 **package (10 ounces) fresh mushrooms, sliced**
¾ **cup chicken broth**
¼ **cup dry red wine *or* water**
3 **tablespoons FRENCH'S® Hearty Deli Brown Mustard**
2 **medium tomatoes, seeded and coarsely chopped**
1 **can (14 ounces) artichoke hearts, drained and quartered**
2 **teaspoons cornstarch**

1. Season chicken with salt and pepper. Heat *1 tablespoon oil* in large nonstick skillet over medium-high heat. Cook chicken 5 minutes or until browned on both sides. Remove and set aside.

2. Heat *1 tablespoon oil* in same skillet until hot. Add mushrooms. Cook and stir 5 minutes or until mushrooms are tender. Stir in broth, wine and mustard. Return chicken to skillet. Add tomatoes and artichoke hearts. Heat to boiling. Reduce heat to medium-low. Cook, covered, 10 minutes or until chicken is no longer pink in center.

3. Combine cornstarch with *1 tablespoon cold water*. Stir into skillet. Heat to boiling. Cook, stirring, over high heat about 1 minute or until sauce thickens. Serve with hot cooked orzo pasta, if desired.   *Makes 4 servings*

Tip

To seed tomatoes, cut them in half crosswise. Gently squeeze tomato halves until seeds come out.

Chicken Rustigo

SAVORY SOUPS & STEWS

Chicken Tortilla Soup

Prep Time: 5 minutes   Cook Time: 6 minutes

- 1 clove garlic, minced
- 1 can (14½ ounces) chicken broth
- 1 jar (16 ounces) mild chunky-style salsa
- 2 tablespoons FRANK'S® REDHOT® Sauce
- 1 package (10 ounces) fully cooked carved chicken breasts
- 1 can (8¾ ounces) whole kernel corn, undrained
- 1 tablespoon chopped fresh cilantro (optional)
- 1 cup crushed tortilla chips
- ½ cup (2 ounces) shredded Monterey Jack cheese

1. Heat *1 teaspoon oil* in large saucepan over medium-high heat. Cook garlic 1 minute or until tender. Add broth, *¾ cup water*, salsa and REDHOT Sauce. Stir in chicken, corn and cilantro. Heat to boiling. Reduce heat to medium-low. Cook, covered, 5 minutes.

2. Stir in tortillas and cheese. Serve hot.

Makes 4 servings

Chicken Tortilla Soup

Cowboy Chili

Prep Time: 15 minutes   Cook Time: 1 hour 15 minutes

- 2 **large onions, chopped**
- 2 **pounds boneless top round *or* sirloin steak, cut into ½-inch cubes**
- 1 **pound ground beef**
- 1 **can (28 ounces) whole tomatoes in purée, undrained**
- 1 **can (15 to 19 ounces) red kidney beans, undrained**
- ⅓ **cup FRANK'S® REDHOT® Sauce**
- 2 **packages (1¼ ounces *each*) chili seasoning mix**

1. Cook and stir onions in *1 tablespoon hot oil* in large pot; transfer to bowl. Cook steak cubes and ground beef in batches in *3 tablespoons hot oil* until well-browned; drain well.

2. Add onions, *¾ cup water* and remaining ingredients to pot. Heat to boiling, stirring. Reduce heat to medium-low. Cook, partially covered, 1 hour or until meat is tender, stirring often. Garnish as desired. *Makes 10 servings*

Ground Beef Variation: Substitute 3 pounds ground beef for the combination of top round and ground beef. Brown meat without oil. Proceed as in step 2. Simmer 20 minutes.

Potato-Cheese Soup

Prep Time: 30 minutes   Cook Time: 25 minutes

- 1½ **cups minced vegetables (celery, carrots, onion)**
- 2 **cloves garlic, minced**
- 2 **pounds peeled red potatoes, cut into ½-inch cubes**
- 4 **cans (14½ ounces *each*) chicken broth**
- ½ **teaspoon ground white pepper**
- ¼ **teaspoon ground red pepper**
- 3 **cups (12 ounces) shredded Cheddar cheese**
- 2 **tablespoons FRENCH'S® Dijon Mustard**
- ¼ **cup minced parsley (optional)**

1. Melt *1 tablespoon butter* in large pot or Dutch oven. Cook and stir celery, carrots, onion and garlic until vegetables are tender. Add potatoes and broth. Cover. Heat to boiling. Reduce heat to medium-low. Cook, partially covered, 15 minutes or until potatoes are tender. Stir occasionally.

2. Combine *1 cup water, ½ cup flour* and peppers in screw-top jar (or mixing bowl); shake (or whisk) until very smooth. Add to vegetables. Cook and stir over medium heat until soup is thickened and bubbly. Gradually add cheese; whisk until cheese melts.

3. Stir in mustard and parsley. Cook and stir over low heat until soup is heated through. Serve with crusty bread or tossed green salad, if desired.   *Makes 6 servings (12 cups)*

Jazzy Jambalaya

Prep Time: 15 minutes   Cook Time: 33 minutes

½ **pound andouille *or* other hot smoked sausage, sliced into ½-inch-thick rounds**
12 **ounces boneless skinless chicken thighs *or* breasts, cut into small cubes**
3 **cups chopped vegetables (onion, green bell pepper, celery)**
1 **can (14½ ounces) whole tomatoes, cut up, undrained**
1 **cup uncooked rice**
¼ **cup FRANK'S® REDHOT® Sauce**

1. Cook sausage in Dutch oven or deep skillet over medium-high heat 5 minutes or until lightly browned. Add chicken; cook and stir 5 minutes or until browned. Add vegetables; cook and stir 3 minutes or until crisp-tender.

2. Stir in *1¼ cups water,* tomatoes, rice, REDHOT Sauce and *½ teaspoon salt.* Heat to boiling. Reduce heat to medium-low. Cook, covered, 20 minutes or until rice is done, stirring once. Garnish with chopped fresh parsley, if desired.

Makes 6 servings

Tip

Leftover cooked chicken, seafood or ham are good additions. Add to recipe in step 2.

Stewed Catfish and Bell Peppers

Prep Time: 15 minutes   Cook Time: 20 minutes

1½ **pounds catfish fillets** *or* **other firm white-fleshed fish**
1 **onion, chopped**
1 *each* **green and red bell pepper, cut into 1-inch pieces**
1 **clove garlic, minced**
1 **cup clam juice**
1 **tomato, chopped**
¼ **cup FRANK'S® REDHOT® Sauce**
2 **tablespoons minced parsley**

1. On sheet of waxed paper, mix *2 tablespoons flour* with *½ teaspoon salt*. Lightly coat fillets with flour mixture; set aside.

2. Heat *1 tablespoon oil* in large nonstick skillet until hot. Add onion, peppers and garlic. Cook and stir 3 minutes or until crisp-tender; transfer to dish.

3. Heat *1 tablespoon oil* in same skillet until hot. Cook fillets 5 minutes or until golden brown, turning once. Return vegetables to skillet. Add clam juice, tomato, REDHOT Sauce and parsley. Heat to boiling. Reduce heat to medium-low. Cook, covered, 8 to 10 minutes or until fish flakes with fork. Serve with hot cooked rice, if desired.   *Makes 6 servings*

Stewed Catfish and Bell Peppers

Minute Minestrone Soup

Prep Time: 10 minutes   Cook Time: about 10 minutes

½ **pound turkey sausage, cut into small pieces**
2 **cloves garlic, crushed**
3 **cans (14½ ounces *each*) low-sodium chicken broth**
2 **cups frozen Italian blend vegetables**
1 **can (15 ounces) white kidney beans, rinsed and drained**
1 **can (14½ ounces) Italian stewed tomatoes, undrained**
1 **cup cooked ditalini *or* small shell pasta (½ cup uncooked)**
3 **tablespoons FRENCH'S® Worcestershire Sauce**

1. In medium saucepan, stir-fry sausage and garlic 5 minutes or until sausage is cooked; drain. Add broth, vegetables, beans and tomatoes. Heat to boiling. Simmer, uncovered, 5 minutes or until vegetables are crisp-tender.

2. Stir in pasta and Worcestershire. Cook until heated through. Serve with grated cheese and crusty bread, if desired.

Makes 6 servings

Chicken Peanut Stew

Prep Time: 10 minutes   Cook Time: 35 minutes

1 (3- to 4-pound) chicken, cut up and skinned, if desired
1 onion, chopped
2 cloves garlic, minced
1 can (6 ounces) tomato paste
½ cup smooth peanut butter
¼ cup FRANK'S® REDHOT® Sauce
1 teaspoon curry powder
2 large carrots, diced

1. Heat *1 tablespoon oil* in large skillet until hot. Add chicken; cook 10 minutes or until browned on both sides. Drain off all but 1 tablespoon fat. Add onion and garlic; cook and stir 3 minutes or until tender.

2. Combine *2 cups water*, tomato paste, peanut butter, REDHOT Sauce and curry powder; whisk until well blended. Pour into skillet. Stir in carrots. Heat to boiling. Reduce heat to medium-low. Cook, partially covered, 20 minutes or until chicken is no longer pink near bone. Serve with hot cooked rice. Garnish with roasted peanuts, if desired.   *Makes 6 servings*

Tip

Devil-up your favorite barbecue sauce—add ¼ cup
FRANK'S REDHOT Sauce to ¾ cup barbecue sauce.

Deviled Beef Short Rib Stew

Prep Time: 20 minutes   Cook Time: about 5 hours

4 **pounds beef short ribs, trimmed**
2 **pounds small red potatoes, scrubbed and scored**
8 **carrots, peeled and cut into chunks**
2 **onions, cut into thick wedges**
1 **bottle (12 ounces) beer** *or* **non-alcoholic malt beverage**
8 **tablespoons FRENCH'S® Hearty Deli Brown Mustard, divided**
3 **tablespoons FRENCH'S® Worcestershire Sauce, divided**
2 **tablespoons cornstarch**

Slow Cooker Directions

1. Broil ribs 6 inches from heat on rack in broiler pan 10 minutes or until well-browned, turning once. Place vegetables in bottom of slow cooker. Place ribs on top of vegetables.

2. Combine beer, *6 tablespoons* mustard and *2 tablespoons* Worcestershire. Pour over all. Cover and cook on high-heat setting 5 hours* or until meat is tender.

3. Transfer meat and vegetables to platter; keep warm. Strain fat from broth; pour broth into saucepan. Combine cornstarch with *2 tablespoons cold water.* Stir into broth with remaining *2 tablespoons* mustard and *1 tablespoon* Worcestershire. Heat to boiling. Reduce heat to medium-low. Cook 1 to 2 minutes or until thickened, stirring often. Pass gravy with meat and vegetables. Serve meat with additional mustard.

Makes 6 servings (with 3 cups gravy)

*Or cook 10 hours on low-heat setting.

Tip

Prepare ingredients the night before for quick assembly in the morning. Keep refrigerated until ready to use.

Deviled Beef Short Rib Stew

Country Smothered Chicken

Prep Time: 5 minutes   Cook Time: 35 minutes

1 (3- to 4-pound) chicken, cut up and skinned, if desired
1 onion, sliced crosswise into rings
1 green bell pepper, chopped
¼ cup FRANK'S® REDHOT® Sauce

1. Place chicken into plastic or brown paper bag. Combine *3 tablespoons flour* with *1 teaspoon salt and ½ teaspoon black pepper.* Sprinkle over chicken pieces. Close bag; shake bag to coat evenly. Heat *1 tablespoon oil* in large nonstick skillet until hot. Add chicken; cook 10 minutes or until browned on both sides. Transfer to dish. Drain off all but 1 tablespoon fat. Add onion and bell pepper; cook and stir 3 minutes or until tender.

2. Slowly add *1 cup water* and REDHOT Sauce; stir until well blended. Heat to boiling. Return chicken to skillet. Reduce heat to medium-low. Cook, partially covered, 20 minutes or until chicken is no longer pink near bone. Serve with hot cooked noodles, if desired. *Makes 6 servings*

Zesty Chicken Succotash

Prep Time: 10 minutes   Cook Time: 35 minutes

- 1 (3- to 4-pound) chicken, cut up and skinned, if desired
- 1 onion, chopped
- 1 rib celery, sliced
- ¼ cup FRANK'S® REDHOT® Sauce
- 1 package (10 ounces) frozen lima beans
- 1 package (10 ounces) frozen whole kernel corn
- 2 tomatoes, coarsely chopped

1. Heat *1 tablespoon oil* in large skillet until hot. Add chicken; cook 10 minutes or until browned on both sides. Drain off all but 1 tablespoon fat. Add onion and celery; cook and stir 3 minutes or until tender.

2. Stir in *¾ cup water*, REDHOT Sauce and remaining ingredients. Heat to boiling. Reduce heat to medium-low. Cook, covered, 20 to 25 minutes or until chicken is no longer pink near bone. Sprinkle with chopped parsley, if desired.   *Makes 6 servings*

Kielbasa and Lentil Stew

Prep Time: 10 minutes   Cook Time: 20 minutes

- 1 pound kielbasa *or* smoked sausage, cut into small cubes
- ½ head green cabbage, shredded (8 cups)
- 1 large onion, chopped
- 4 carrots, shredded
- 2 cans (19 ounces *each*) lentil soup
- 1 can (16 ounces) crushed tomatoes in purée, undrained
- 3 tablespoons FRANK'S® REDHOT® Sauce

1. Cook and stir sausage in 5-quart saucepot over medium-high heat 3 minutes or until lightly browned. Add vegetables; cook and stir 5 minutes or until tender.

2. Stir in soup, tomatoes and REDHOT Sauce. Heat to boiling. Reduce heat to medium-low. Cook, partially covered, 10 minutes or until heated through and flavors are blended. Ladle stew into bowls.   *Makes 8 to 10 servings*

Hearty Ground Beef Stew

Prep Time: 5 minutes   Cook Time: 15 minutes

1 pound ground beef
3 cloves garlic, minced
1 package (16 ounces) Italian-style frozen vegetables
2 cups southern-style hash brown potatoes
1 jar (14 ounces) marinara sauce
1 can (10½ ounces) condensed beef broth
3 tablespoons FRENCH'S® Worcestershire Sauce

1. Brown beef with garlic in large saucepan; drain. Add remaining ingredients. Heat to boiling. Cover. Reduce heat to medium-low. Cook 10 minutes or until vegetables are crisp-tender.

2. Serve in warm bowls with garlic bread, if desired.

Makes 6 servings

Brazilian Black Bean Soup

Prep Time: 10 minutes   Cook Time: 30 minutes

1 red onion, chopped
2 cloves garlic, minced
1 can (29 ounces) black beans, drained
1 can (14½ ounces) vegetable *or* chicken broth
3 tablespoons FRANK'S® REDHOT® Sauce
2 tablespoons chopped cilantro
2 teaspoons ground cumin
2 tablespoons rum *or* sherry (optional)

1. Heat *1 tablespoon oil* in 3-quart saucepot. Cook and stir onion and garlic 3 minutes or just until tender. Stir in *1½ cups water* and remaining ingredients *except* rum. Heat to boiling. Reduce heat to medium-low. Cook, partially covered, 20 minutes or until flavors are blended, stirring occasionally.

2. Ladle about half of soup into blender or food processor. Cover securely. Process on low speed until mixture is smooth. Return to saucepot. Stir in rum. Cook over medium-low heat 3 minutes or until heated through and flavors are blended. Garnish with lime slices, sour cream, minced onion or cilantro, if desired.

Makes 4 to 6 servings

Hearty Ground Beef Stew

French Quarter Shrimp Creole

Prep Time: 10 minutes   Cook Time: 15 minutes

½ **cup** *each* **chopped onion, celery and green bell pepper**
1 **clove garlic, minced**
1 **can (14½ ounces) stewed tomatoes, undrained**
¼ **cup FRANK'S® REDHOT® Sauce**
1 **pound medium shrimp, peeled and deveined**
   Hot cooked rice

1. Melt *2 tablespoons butter* in medium skillet; blend in *2 tablespoons flour.* Add onion, celery, bell pepper and garlic; cook and stir over medium-high heat 5 minutes or until vegetables are tender and flour mixture is lightly golden.

2. Stir in tomatoes and REDHOT Sauce. Heat to boiling. Reduce heat to medium-low. Cook, uncovered, 5 minutes or until slightly thickened. Stir occasionally. Add shrimp. Cook 5 minutes or just until shrimp are pink. Serve over rice. Garnish with chopped parsley, if desired. *Makes 4 servings*

Pork & Vegetable Hot Pot

Prep Time: 5 minutes   Cook Time: about 5 minutes

½ **pound boneless loin pork chops, cut into very thin strips**
¼ **cup FRANK'S® REDHOT® Sauce**
1 **can (10½ ounces) condensed beef broth**
1 **package (16 ounces) frozen stir-fry vegetables**
1 **cup uncooked medium egg noodles**
1 **green onion, sliced**

1. Combine pork and REDHOT Sauce in medium bowl; set aside.

2. Combine broth and *2½ cups water* in large saucepan. Heat to boiling. Add vegetables and noodles; return to boiling. Cook 2 minutes. Stir in pork and green onion. Cook 1 minute or until pork is cooked. *Makes 4 servings*

Asian Pasta & Shrimp Soup

Prep Time: 10 minutes   Cook Time: about 10 minutes

- 1 **package (3½ ounces) fresh shiitake mushrooms**
- 2 **teaspoons Oriental sesame oil**
- 2 **cans (14½ ounces** *each***) vegetable broth**
- 4 **ounces angel-hair pasta, broken into 2-inch lengths (about 1 cup)**
- ½ **pound medium shrimp, peeled and deveined**
- 4 **ounces snow peas, cut into thin strips**
- 2 **tablespoons FRENCH'S® Dijon Mustard**
- 1 **tablespoon FRANK'S® REDHOT® Sauce**
- ⅛ **teaspoon ground ginger**

1. Remove and discard stems from mushrooms. Cut mushrooms into thin strips. Heat oil in large saucepan over medium-high heat. Add mushrooms; stir-fry 3 minutes or just until tender.

2. Add broth and ½ *cup water* to saucepan. Heat to boiling. Stir in pasta. Cook 2 minutes or just until tender.

3. Add remaining ingredients, stirring frequently. Heat to boiling. Reduce heat to medium-low. Cook 2 minutes or until shrimp turn pink and peas are tender.   *Makes 4 servings*

MEATY SALADS & MEATLESS ENTRÉES

Creamy Mashed Potato Bake

Prep Time: 5 minutes   Cook Time: 35 minutes

- 3 **cups mashed potatoes**
- 1 **cup sour cream**
- ¼ **cup milk**
- ¼ **teaspoon garlic powder**
- 1⅓ **cups FRENCH'S® Taste Toppers™ French Fried Onions, divided**
- 1 **cup (4 ounces) shredded Cheddar cheese, divided**

1. Preheat oven to 350°F. Combine mashed potatoes, sour cream, milk and garlic powder.

2. Spoon half of mixture into 2-quart casserole. Sprinkle with ⅔ *cup* Taste Toppers and ½ *cup* cheese. Top with remaining potato mixture.

3. Bake 30 minutes or until hot. Top with remaining ⅔ *cup* onions and ½ *cup* cheese. Bake 5 minutes or until onions are golden.

Makes 6 servings

Creamy Mashed Potato Bake

Beef Caesar Salad

Prep Time: 35 minutes   Cook Time: 15 minutes

2 **pounds boneless beef sirloin, top round or flank steak**
1 **bottle (8 ounces) creamy Caesar salad dressing**
¼ **cup FRENCH'S® Worcestershire Sauce**
¼ **cup FRENCH'S® Dijon Mustard**
1 **teaspoon grated lemon peel**
2 **tablespoons lemon juice**
8 **cups romaine lettuce leaves, washed and torn**

1. Place steak in resealable plastic food storage bag. Combine remaining ingredients *except* lettuce. Pour ¾ *cup* sauce over steak. Seal bag; marinate steak in refrigerator 30 minutes. Reserve remaining sauce for dressing.

2. Broil steak 15 minutes for medium-rare. Let stand 15 minutes. Slice steak; serve with dressing over lettuce.   *Makes 8 servings*

Upside-Down Cornbread

Prep Time: 10 minutes   Cook Time: 35 minutes

3 **plum tomatoes, thinly sliced**
1⅓ **cups FRENCH'S® Taste Toppers™ French Fried Onions, divided**
2 **packages (6½ ounces *each*) cornbread mix**
2 **eggs**
⅔ **cup milk**
¼ **cup butter, melted**
½ **cup finely chopped zucchini**
1 **teaspoon FRENCH'S® Hearty Deli Brown Mustard**
½ **teaspoon dried basil leaves**

1. Preheat oven to 425°F. Coat 8-inch square baking pan with nonstick cooking spray. Layer tomatoes in bottom of pan and sprinkle with ⅓ *cup* Taste Toppers. Bake 5 minutes.

2. Combine *1 cup* onions and remaining ingredients in medium bowl; mix just until dry ingredients are moistened. Pour over tomato layers. Bake 30 minutes or until toothpick inserted in center comes out clean. Cool 15 minutes; invert onto serving plate. Serve warm with tossed green salad.   *Makes 6 servings*

Beef Caesar Salad

Citrus-Berry Chicken Salad

Prep Time: 10 minutes   Cook Time: 10 minutes

- 4 **boneless skinless chicken breast halves**
- ½ **cup FRENCH'S® Honey Mustard, divided**
- ⅓ **cup canola oil**
- 2 **tablespoons raspberry vinegar *or* balsamic vinegar**
- 8 **cups mixed salad greens, washed and torn**
- 1 **cup sliced strawberries *or* raspberries**
- 1 **orange, cut into sections**

1. Coat chicken with ¼ *cup* mustard. Broil or grill 10 to 15 minutes or until chicken is no longer pink in center. Cut diagonally into slices.

2. In small bowl, whisk together remaining ¼ *cup* mustard, oil, vinegar and ¼ *teaspoon each salt and pepper.*

3. Arrange salad greens and fruit on serving plates. Top with chicken. Drizzle with dressing just before serving.

Makes 4 servings

Fiesta Potato Bake

Prep Time: 10 minutes   Cook Time: 48 minutes

- 1 **package (32 ounces) frozen southern-style hash brown potatoes**
- 1⅓ **cups FRENCH'S® Taste Toppers™ French Fried Onions, divided**
- 2 **cups (8 ounces) shredded Cheddar *or* Monterey Jack cheese, divided**
- 1 **can (10¾ ounces) condensed cream of celery *or* chicken soup**
- 2 **cans (4½ ounces *each*) chopped mild green chilies, undrained**
- 1 **cup sour cream**
- 2 **eggs, beaten**
- 2 **tablespoons FRANK'S® REDHOT® Sauce**

1. Preheat oven to 400°F. Layer potatoes, ⅔ *cup* Taste Toppers and *1 cup* cheese in 3-quart shallow casserole. Combine soup, chilies, sour cream, eggs and REDHOT Sauce in medium bowl. Pour over potatoes; stir.

2. Bake, uncovered, 45 minutes or until potatoes are cooked and mixture is set.

3. Sprinkle with remaining *1 cup* cheese and ⅔ *cup* onions. Bake 3 minutes or until onions are golden. Garnish with diced pimiento, if desired.   *Makes 6 servings*

Crustless Asparagus Quiche

Prep Time: 10 minutes   Cook Time: 35 minutes

- ½ **pound fresh asparagus, trimmed and cut into ½-inch pieces**
- 1½ **cups (6 ounces) shredded Swiss cheese, divided**
- 1⅓ **cups FRENCH'S® Taste Toppers™ French Fried Onions, divided**
- 6 **eggs**
- ½ **cup milk**
- ½ **cup (2 ounces) grated Parmesan cheese**
- ¼ **teaspoon garlic powder**

1. Preheat oven to 350°F. Grease 9-inch deep-dish pie plate. Arrange asparagus, *1 cup* Swiss cheese and ⅔ *cup* Taste Toppers in plate.

2. Beat eggs, milk, Parmesan cheese, *1 tablespoon flour*, garlic powder and ⅛ *teaspoon pepper* in medium bowl. Pour into prepared pie plate.

3. Bake 30 minutes or just until center is set. Sprinkle with remaining ½ *cup* Swiss cheese and ⅔ *cup* onions. Bake 5 minutes or until onions are golden. Cut into wedges to serve.

Makes 6 servings

Tip

You may substitute 1 (10-ounce) package thawed frozen asparagus spears, cut into ½-inch pieces.

Vegetarian Chili with Cornbread Topping

Prep Time: 20 minutes   Cook Time: 35 minutes

- 1 pound zucchini, halved and cut into ½-inch slices (about 4 cups)
- 1 red *or* green bell pepper, cut into 1-inch pieces
- 1 rib celery, thinly sliced
- 1 clove garlic, minced
- 2 cans (15 to 19 ounces *each*) kidney beans, rinsed and drained
- 1 can (28 ounces) crushed tomatoes in purée, undrained
- ¼ cup FRANK'S® REDHOT® Sauce
- 1 tablespoon chili powder
- 1 package (6½ ounces) cornbread mix plus ingredients to prepare mix

1. Preheat oven to 400°F. Heat *1 tablespoon oil* in 12-inch heatproof skillet* over medium-high heat. Add zucchini, bell pepper, celery and garlic. Cook and stir 5 minutes or until tender. Stir in beans, tomatoes, REDHOT Sauce and chili powder. Heat to boiling, stirring.

2. Prepare cornbread mix according to package directions. Spoon batter on top of chili mixture, spreading to ½ inch from edges. Bake 30 minutes or until cornbread is golden brown and mixture is bubbly.   *Makes 6 servings*

If handle of skillet is not heatproof, wrap in foil.

Tip

Salsa Olé! Spike up the flavor of salsa by adding FRANK'S REDHOT Sauce to taste. Serve with chips or on top of fajitas and tacos.

Vegetarian Chili with Cornbread Topping

Crunchy Layered Beef & Bean Salad

Prep Time: 10 minutes   Cook Time: 6 minutes

- 1 **pound ground beef** *or* **turkey**
- 2 **cans (15 to 19 ounces** *each***) black beans** *or* **pinto beans, rinsed and drained**
- 1 **can (14½ ounces) stewed tomatoes, undrained**
- 1⅓ **cups FRENCH'S® Taste Toppers™ French Fried Onions, divided**
- 1 **package (1¼ ounces) taco seasoning mix**
- 6 **cups shredded lettuce**
- 1 **cup (4 ounces) shredded Cheddar** *or* **Monterey Jack cheese**

1. In large nonstick skillet, cook beef until thoroughly browned; drain well. Stir in beans, tomatoes, ⅔ *cup* Taste Toppers and taco seasoning. Heat to boiling. Cook over medium heat 5 minutes, stirring occasionally.

2. Spoon beef mixture over lettuce on serving platter. Top with cheese.

3. Microwave remaining ⅔ *cup* onions 1 minute on HIGH. Sprinkle over salad.   *Makes 6 servings*

Pasta with Spicy Tomato Sauce

Prep Time: 10 minutes   Cook Time: 15 minutes

- 8 **whole cloves garlic, peeled**
- 1 **can (28 ounces) crushed tomatoes in purée, undrained**
- ½ **cup chopped black olives**
- ¼ **cup FRANK'S® REDHOT® Sauce**
- ¼ **cup minced basil** *or* **parsley**
- 1 **tablespoon capers (optional)**
- 4 **cups hot cooked tube-shaped pasta**

1. Heat *2 tablespoons oil* in large skillet; cook and stir garlic until lightly golden. Add remaining ingredients *except* pasta. Heat to boiling. Simmer, stirring, 10 minutes.

2. In serving bowl, toss pasta with half of sauce. Serve remaining sauce on the side. Garnish with shredded cheese, if desired.

Makes 4 servings (3 cups sauce)

Crunchy Layered Beef & Bean Salad

Mandarin Steak Salad

Prep Time: 10 minutes   Cook Time: 10 minutes

⅓ cup FRENCH'S® Hearty Deli Brown Mustard
2 tablespoons teriyaki sauce
1 tablespoon sugar
½ teaspoon garlic powder
½ teaspoon ground ginger
1 can (11 ounces) mandarin oranges, *reserve ¼ cup liquid*
1 pound boneless sirloin steak (1 inch thick)
8 cups mixed salad greens, washed and torn
2 green onions, thinly shredded
⅓ cup dry roasted peanuts, chopped

1. Combine mustard, teriyaki sauce, sugar, garlic powder and ginger in small bowl. Stir in reserved mandarin orange liquid. Pour *½ cup* dressing into serving bowl.

2. Brush remaining dressing on steak. Broil or grill steak 10 minutes or until desired doneness. Let stand 5 minutes.

3. Thinly slice steak. Serve over salad greens. Top with oranges, green onions and peanuts. Drizzle with reserved dressing.

Makes 4 servings

Italian Vegetable Strata

Prep Time: 10 minutes   Cook Time: 50 minutes

1 loaf Italian bread
1⅓ cups FRENCH'S® Taste Toppers™ French Fried Onions, divided
1 cup (4 ounces) shredded mozzarella cheese, divided
1 small zucchini, thinly sliced
1 red bell pepper, sliced
5 eggs
2½ cups milk
⅓ cup (1½ ounces) grated Parmesan cheese
½ teaspoon *each* dried oregano and basil leaves

1. Preheat oven to 350°F. Grease 3-quart shallow baking dish. Cut enough slices of bread, ½ inch thick, to arrange single layer in bottom of dish, overlapping slices if necessary. Layer ⅔ *cup* Taste Toppers, ⅔ *cup* mozzarella cheese, zucchini and bell pepper over bread.

2. Beat eggs, milk, Parmesan cheese, oregano, basil, ½ *teaspoon salt* and ¼ *teaspoon black pepper* in medium bowl. Pour over layers. Sprinkle with remaining ⅓ *cup* mozzarella cheese. Let stand 10 minutes.

3. Bake 45 minutes or until knife inserted in center comes out clean. Sprinkle with remaining ⅔ *cup* onions. Bake 5 minutes or until onions are golden. Cool on wire rack 10 minutes. Cut into squares to serve. *Makes 8 servings*

Fireball Vegetarian Chili

Prep Time: 15 minutes   Cook Time: 25 minutes

    1 onion, chopped
    2 cloves garlic, minced
    2 cans (15 to 19 ounces *each*) red kidney beans, rinsed
        and drained
 1½ cups *each* coarsely chopped zucchini and carrots
    1 can (15 ounces) crushed tomatoes in purée, undrained
    1 can (7 ounces) whole kernel corn, drained
    1 can (4½ ounces) chopped green chilies, drained
    ¼ cup FRANK'S® REDHOT® Sauce
    1 tablespoon ground cumin

1. Heat *1 tablespoon oil* in large saucepot. Cook and stir onion and garlic 3 minutes or just until tender. Add remaining ingredients; stir until well blended.

2. Heat to boiling. Reduce heat to medium-low. Cook, partially covered, 20 minutes or until vegetables are tender and flavors are blended. Serve with hot cooked rice. Garnish with sour cream or shredded cheese, if desired. *Makes 6 servings*

Tip

Serve chili over hot baked potatoes.

Savory Roasted Vegetables & Pasta

Prep Time: 20 minutes   Cook Time: 20 minutes

4 **carrots, thinly sliced**
2 **red bell peppers, cut into strips**
2 **zucchini, cut into ½-inch chunks**
2 **yellow squash, cut into ½-inch chunks**
4 **cloves garlic, peeled**
½ **cup half-and-half**
3 **tablespoons FRENCH'S® Dijon Mustard**
8 **ounces penne pasta, cooked**
   Shaved Parmesan cheese

1. Preheat oven to 425°F. In roasting pan, toss vegetables and garlic with *2 tablespoons olive oil, 1 teaspoon salt* and *¼ teaspoon black pepper*. Bake, uncovered, 20 minutes or until tender, stirring occasionally.

2. Spoon half of vegetables into blender or food processor. Add half-and-half, mustard and *2 tablespoons water*. Process until mixture is smooth.

3. Toss pasta with vegetable purée in large serving bowl. Spoon remaining vegetables on top. Sprinkle with Parmesan cheese.

Makes 4 servings

Reuben Salad

Prep Time: 15 minutes

½ **cup Italian salad dressing**
¼ **cup FRENCH'S® Hearty Deli Brown Mustard**
½ **pound Swiss cheese**
½ **pound pastrami** *or* **corned beef**
3 **cooked medium red potatoes**
2 **cups sauerkraut, drained**
⅔ **cup finely chopped dill pickles**

1. Combine dressing and mustard in large bowl.

2. Cut cheese, pastrami and potatoes into ½-inch cubes. Add to dressing in bowl with sauerkraut and pickles; toss to coat. Serve with crusty pumpernickel bread. Serve on bed of cabbage or lettuce leaves, if desired.

Makes 6 servings

Savory Roasted Vegetables & Pasta

Balsamic Chicken Salad

Prep Time: 10 minutes

⅓ cup olive oil
¼ cup FRENCH'S® Honey Mustard
2 tablespoons balsamic *or* red wine vinegar
1 teaspoon minced shallots *or* onion
8 cups mixed salad greens, washed and torn
1 package (10 ounces) fully cooked carved chicken breasts
1 package (4 ounces) goat *or* Feta cheese, crumbled
1 cup croutons

1. Whisk together oil, mustard, vinegar, shallots, *2 tablespoons water* and *⅛ teaspoon salt*.

2. Arrange salad greens, chicken, cheese and croutons on serving plates. Serve with dressing.   *Makes 4 servings*

Quick Black Beans & Yellow Rice

Prep Time: 5 minutes   Cook Time: 15 minutes

1 small onion, chopped
½ cup chopped green bell pepper
2 cloves garlic, minced
2 cans (15 to 19 ounces *each*) black beans, undrained
¼ cup FRANK'S® REDHOT® Sauce
1 teaspoon dried oregano leaves
1 bay leaf
Yellow Rice (recipe follows)

1. Heat *1 tablespoon oil* in large saucepan over medium-high heat. Cook and stir onion, bell pepper and garlic 3 minutes or until tender.

2. Stir in beans, REDHOT Sauce and herbs. Cook 10 minutes over medium heat or until beans are heated through and flavors are blended, stirring occasionally. Discard bay leaf. Serve over Yellow Rice. Garnish with minced cilantro, if desired.

Makes 6 servings

Yellow Rice: Add ¼ teaspoon turmeric to cooking water for 1 cup white rice or 2 bags boil-in-bag rice.

Balsamic Chicken Salad

SUPER SANDWICHES & WRAPS

Quick 'n' Easy Tacos

Prep Time: 5 minutes   Cook Time: 10 minutes

- **1 pound ground beef** *or* **turkey**
- **1 cup salsa**
- **¼ cup FRANK'S® REDHOT® Sauce**
- **2 teaspoons ground chili powder**
- **8 taco shells, heated**
- **Garnish: chopped tomatoes, shredded lettuce, sliced olives, sour cream, shredded cheese**

1. Cook beef in skillet over medium-high heat 5 minutes or until browned, stirring to separate meat; drain. Stir in salsa, REDHOT Sauce and chili powder. Heat to boiling. Reduce heat to medium-low. Cook 5 minutes, stirring often.

2. To serve, spoon meat mixture into taco shells. Splash on more REDHOT Sauce to taste. Garnish as desired. *Makes 4 servings*

Quick 'n' Easy Tacos

Smokin' Beef Fajitas

Prep Time: 15 minutes   Cook Time: 15 minutes

1½ **pounds lean flank steak *or* top round steak**
½ **cup FRANK'S® REDHOT® Sauce**
½ **cup smoky-flavored barbecue sauce**
2 **teaspoons ground cumin**
2 **green *or* red bell peppers, cut into strips**
1 **large onion, cut into ¼-inch wedges**
Heated flour tortillas

1. Cut steak into 3×1×¼-inch slices; place in large bowl. Combine REDHOT Sauce, barbecue sauce and cumin. Pour ⅓ *cup* sauce over steak; toss to coat. Let stand 5 minutes. Reserve remaining sauce mixture.

2. Heat *1 tablespoon oil* in large nonstick skillet until hot. Stir-fry vegetables 5 minutes or until tender. Transfer to clean bowl.

3. Heat *1 to 2 tablespoons oil* in same skillet over high heat until very hot. Stir-fry steak in batches until browned. Transfer steak and any pan juices to bowl with vegetables. Return all to skillet. Stir in reserved sauce mixture; toss to coat. Cook until heated through. Serve in tortillas.   *Makes 6 servings*

Broiled Vegetable Focaccia

Prep Time: 10 minutes   Cook Time: 12 minutes

4 **(6-inch) prepared Italian pizza crusts (4 ounces *each*)**
3 **tablespoons FRENCH'S® Dijon Mustard**
3 **tablespoons reduced-fat mayonnaise**
1 **teaspoon dried basil leaves *or* 1 tablespoon minced fresh basil**
1 **red bell pepper, coarsely chopped**
1 **yellow squash, coarsely chopped**
1 **zucchini, coarsely chopped**
¼ **cup grated Parmesan cheese**

1. Preheat broiler. Place crusts in broiler pan. Heat 1 minute or until toasted. Transfer to work surface. Combine mustard, mayonnaise and basil. Spread evenly on top of crusts.

2. Toss vegetables with *2 tablespoons oil* and *½ teaspoon salt.* Place on broiling pan. Broil 6 inches from heat 10 minutes or until vegetables are crisp-tender and slightly charred, turning once.

3. Arrange vegetables on top of prepared crusts. Sprinkle with cheese. Heat under broiler 1 minute or until cheese turns golden.

Makes 4 servings

Fiesta Burritos

Prep Time: 5 minutes	Cook Time: 5 minutes

1 **can (16 ounces) fat-free refried beans**
¼ **cup FRANK'S® REDHOT® Sauce**
2 **teaspoons ground cumin**
8 **(8-inch) flour tortillas, heated**
2 **cups assorted fillings (scrambled eggs, cooked rice,**
   diced cooked chicken *or* pork *or* shredded beef)
   Garnish: salsa, chopped tomatoes, sour cream, chopped
   green onions

1. Combine refried beans, REDHOT Sauce and cumin in medium saucepan. Cook and stir over medium-high heat 5 minutes or until hot and flavors are blended.

2. Spoon about *3 tablespoons* bean mixture in center of each tortilla. Top with *¼ cup* desired filling. Fold into burritos. Garnish as desired.

Makes 4 servings

Tip

- Folding Burritos: Place filling in center of tortilla. Fold bottom third of tortilla over filling. Fold over both sides of tortilla. Roll up to enclose filling.
- To Heat Tortillas: Place tortillas in damp microwave-safe paper towel. Microwave on HIGH 1 to 2 minutes or until heated through.
- If desired, assorted fillings may be omitted. Garnish as desired before filling with bean mixture.

Garlic Roast Beef Subs

Prep Time: 10 minutes   Cook Time: about 10 minutes

2 **cups thinly sliced onions**
3 **tablespoons FRENCH'S® Worcestershire Sauce**
1 **container (4 ounces) garlic-flavored cheese spread**
4 **sandwich rolls, split in half and toasted**
12 **ounces sliced deli roast beef**

1. Melt *1 tablespoon butter* in medium skillet over medium-high heat. Add onions; cook and stir 5 minutes or until tender. Add Worcestershire; cook 2 minutes.

2. Spread about *1 tablespoon* cheese on each half of rolls. Broil 30 seconds or until cheese begins to brown. Layer roast beef and onions on bottoms of rolls. Cover with top halves.

Makes 4 servings

Sautéed Pork Peperonata

Prep Time: 10 minutes   Cook Time: 10 minutes

1 **pound boneless loin pork chops, cut into thin strips**
3 **cloves garlic, minced**
1 **onion, sliced**
1 *each* **green and red bell pepper, cut into 1-inch chunks**
½ **teaspoon dried basil leaves**
4 **tablespoons FRANK'S® REDHOT® Sauce, divided**
4 **large rolls, split**

1. Combine pork and garlic. Heat *1 tablespoon oil* in large nonstick skillet over medium-high heat until hot. Cook pork mixture 3 minutes or until browned; remove from skillet.

2. Heat *1 tablespoon oil* in same skillet. Add vegetables, basil and *1 tablespoon* REDHOT Sauce. Cook, covered, 5 minutes, stirring occasionally.

3. Return pork to skillet; add remaining *3 tablespoons* REDHOT Sauce. Cook, covered, 1 minute. Serve on rolls.

Makes 4 servings

Garlic Roast Beef Sub

BBQ Pork Sandwiches

Prep Time: 10 minutes   Cook Time: 5 hours

4 **pounds boneless pork loin roast, fat trimmed**
1 **can (14½ ounces) beef broth**
⅓ **cup FRENCH'S® Worcestershire Sauce**
⅓ **cup FRANK'S® REDHOT® Sauce**

SAUCE
½ **cup ketchup**
½ **cup molasses**
¼ **cup FRENCH'S® CLASSIC YELLOW® Mustard**
¼ **cup FRENCH'S® Worcestershire Sauce**
2 **tablespoons FRANK'S® REDHOT® Sauce**

Slow Cooker Directions

1. Place roast in bottom of slow cooker. Combine broth, ⅓ cup *each* Worcestershire and REDHOT Sauce. Pour over roast. Cover and cook on high-heat setting 5 hours* or until roast is tender.

2. Meanwhile, combine ingredients for sauce in large bowl; set aside.

3. Transfer roast to large cutting board. Discard liquid. Coarsely chop roast. Stir into reserved sauce. Spoon pork mixture on large rolls. Serve with deli potato salad, if desired.

Makes 8 to 10 servings

*Or cook 10 hours on low-heat setting.

Tip

Make additional sauce and serve on the side. Great also with barbecued ribs and chops!

BBQ Pork Sandwich

Spicy Sausage Heroes

Prep Time: 10 minutes   Cook Time: 30 minutes

- 1 **pound Italian sausage**
- 1 **onion, thinly sliced**
- 1 **green bell pepper, cut into strips**
- 2 **cloves garlic, chopped**
- 1 **can (14½ ounces) stewed tomatoes, undrained**
- 2 **tablespoons FRENCH'S® Hearty Deli Brown Mustard**
- 1 **tablespoon FRENCH'S® Worcestershire Sauce**
- 4 **crusty Italian-style rolls, split and toasted**
- ½ **cup (4 ounces) shredded mozzarella cheese**

1. Cook sausage in large nonstick skillet over medium-high heat 20 minutes or until browned and cooked in center. Drain fat. Cut sausage into ½-inch pieces; set aside.

2. Heat *1 tablespoon oil* in same skillet until hot. Cook and stir onion, bell pepper and garlic 5 minutes or until tender. Add tomatoes, mustard and Worcestershire. Return sausage to skillet. Heat to boiling, stirring. Reduce heat to medium-low. Cook 5 minutes or until sauce thickens slightly and flavors are blended.

3. Spoon sausage mixture into rolls, dividing evenly. Top with cheese. Serve warm.   *Makes 4 servings*

Sloppy Joes

Prep Time: 5 minutes   Cook Time: 10 minutes

- 1 **pound ground beef *or* turkey**
- 1 **can (10¾ ounces) condensed tomato soup**
- 2 **tablespoons FRENCH'S® Worcestershire Sauce**
- 4 **large rolls, split**
  Garnish: shredded Cheddar cheese, sliced green onions, chopped tomatoes

1. Cook beef in large skillet until browned; drain. Add soup, *¼ cup water* and Worcestershire. Heat to boiling. Simmer over low heat 5 minutes, stirring often.

2. Serve in rolls. Top with cheese, onions and tomatoes.

Makes 4 servings

All-Time Favorite
Casseroles

All-Time Favorite Casseroles

pg. 166

pg. 206

pg. 234

Daybreak Delights

Summer Sausage 'n' Egg Wedges

 4 eggs, beaten
⅓ cup milk
¼ cup all-purpose flour
½ teaspoon baking powder
⅛ teaspoon garlic powder
2½ cups (10 ounces) shredded
    Cheddar or mozzarella
    cheese, divided
1½ cups diced HILLSHIRE FARM®
    Summer Sausage
 1 cup cream-style cottage
    cheese with chives

Preheat oven to 375°F.

Combine eggs, milk, flour, baking powder and garlic powder in medium bowl; beat until combined. Stir in 2 cups Cheddar cheese, Summer Sausage and cottage cheese. Pour into greased 9-inch pie plate. Bake, uncovered, 25 to 30 minutes or until golden and knife inserted into center comes out clean. To serve, cut into 6 wedges. Sprinkle wedges with remaining ½ cup Cheddar cheese.

Makes 6 servings

pg. 164

pg. 172

Summer Sausage 'n' Egg Wedge

Brunch Eggs Olé

8 eggs
½ cup all-purpose flour
1 teaspoon baking powder
¾ teaspoon salt
2 cups (8 ounces) shredded Monterey Jack cheese with jalapeño peppers
1½ cups (12 ounces) small curd cottage cheese
1 cup (4 ounces) shredded sharp Cheddar cheese
1 jalapeño pepper,* seeded and chopped
½ teaspoon hot pepper sauce
Fresh Salsa (recipe follows)

*Jalapeño peppers can sting and irritate the skin; wear rubber gloves when handling peppers and do not touch eyes. Wash hands after handling.

1. Preheat oven to 350°F. Grease 9-inch square baking pan.

2. Beat eggs in large bowl with electric mixer at high speed 4 to 5 minutes or until slightly thickened and lemon-colored.

3. Combine flour, baking powder and salt in small bowl. Stir flour mixture into eggs until blended.

4. Combine Monterey Jack cheese, cottage cheese, Cheddar cheese, jalapeño pepper and hot pepper sauce in medium bowl; mix well. Fold into egg mixture until well blended. Pour into prepared pan.

5. Bake 45 to 50 minutes or until golden brown and firm in center. Let stand 10 minutes before cutting into squares. Serve with Fresh Salsa. Garnish as desired.
Makes 8 servings

Fresh Salsa

3 medium plum tomatoes, seeded and chopped
2 tablespoons chopped onion
1 small jalapeño pepper,* seeded and minced
1 tablespoon chopped fresh cilantro
1 tablespoon lime juice
¼ teaspoon salt
⅛ teaspoon black pepper

*Jalapeño peppers can sting and irritate the skin; wear rubber gloves when handling peppers and do not touch eyes. Wash hands after handling.

Stir together tomatoes, onion, jalapeño pepper, cilantro, lime juice, salt and black pepper in small bowl. Refrigerate until ready to serve. *Makes 1 cup*

Brunch Eggs Olé

Low Fat Turkey Bacon Frittata

1 package (12 ounces)
    BUTTERBALL® Turkey
    Bacon, heated and chopped
6 ounces uncooked angel hair
    pasta, broken
2 teaspoons olive oil
1 small onion, sliced
1 red bell pepper, cut into thin
    strips
4 containers (4 ounces each)
    egg substitute
1 container (5 ounces) fat free
    ricotta cheese
1 cup (4 ounces) shredded fat
    free mozzarella cheese
1 cup (4 ounces) shredded
    reduced fat Swiss cheese
½ teaspoon salt
½ teaspoon black pepper
1 package (10 ounces) frozen
    spinach, thawed and
    squeezed dry

Cook and drain pasta. Heat oil in large skillet over medium heat until hot. Cook and stir onion and bell pepper until tender. Combine egg substitute, cheeses, salt, black pepper and cooked pasta in large bowl. Add vegetables, spinach and turkey bacon. Spray 10-inch quiche dish with nonstick cooking spray; pour mixture into dish. Bake in preheated 350°F oven 30 minutes. Cut into wedges. Serve with spicy salsa, if desired.

Makes 8 servings

Ham & Cheese Grits Soufflé

 3 cups water
¾ cup quick-cooking grits
½ teaspoon salt
½ cup (2 ounces) shredded
    mozzarella cheese
 2 ounces ham, finely chopped
 2 tablespoons minced chives
 2 eggs, separated
    Dash hot pepper sauce

1. Preheat oven to 375°F. Grease 1½-quart soufflé dish or deep casserole.

2. Bring water to a boil in medium saucepan. Stir in grits and salt. Cook, stirring frequently, about 5 minutes or until thickened. Stir in cheese, ham, chives, egg yolks and hot pepper sauce.

3. In small clean bowl, beat egg whites until stiff but not dry; fold into grits mixture. Pour into prepared dish. Bake about 30 minutes or until puffed and golden. Serve immediately.

Makes 4 to 6 servings

Low Fat Turkey Bacon Frittata

Cheddar Cheese Strata

1 pound French bread, cut into
½- to ¾-inch slices, crusts
removed, divided
2 cups (8 ounces) shredded
reduced-fat Cheddar
cheese, divided
2 whole eggs
3 egg whites
1 quart fat-free (skim) milk
1 teaspoon dry mustard
1 teaspoon grated fresh onion
½ teaspoon salt
Paprika to taste

1. Spray 13×9-inch glass baking dish with nonstick cooking spray. Place half the bread slices in bottom of prepared dish, overlapping slightly. Sprinkle with 1¼ cups cheese. Place remaining bread slices on top of cheese.

2. Whisk whole eggs and egg whites in large bowl. Add milk, mustard, onion and salt; whisk until well blended. Pour evenly over bread and cheese. Cover with remaining ¾ cup cheese and sprinkle with paprika. Cover and refrigerate 1 hour or overnight.

3. Preheat oven to 350°F. Bake about 45 minutes or until cheese is melted and bread is golden brown. Let stand 5 minutes before serving. Garnish with red bell pepper stars and fresh Italian parsley, if desired.

Makes 8 servings

Lit'l Links Soufflé

8 slices white bread
2 cups (8 ounces) shredded
Cheddar cheese
1 pound HILLSHIRE FARM®
Lit'l Polskas
6 eggs
2¾ cups milk
¾ teaspoon dry mustard

Spread bread in bottom of greased 13×9-inch baking pan. Sprinkle cheese over top of bread.

Arrange Lit'l Polskas on top of cheese. Beat eggs with milk and mustard in large bowl; pour over links. Cover pan with aluminum foil; refrigerate overnight.

Preheat oven to 300°F. Bake egg mixture 1½ hours or until puffy and brown.

Makes 4 to 6 servings

Chiles Rellenos en Casserole

3 eggs, separated
¾ cup milk
¾ cup all-purpose flour
½ teaspoon salt
1 tablespoon butter or margarine
½ cup chopped onion
8 peeled roasted whole chiles *or* 2 cans (7 ounces each) whole green chiles, drained
8 ounces Monterey Jack cheese, cut into 8 strips

CONDIMENTS
Sour cream
Sliced green onions
Pitted black olive slices
Guacamole
Salsa

Preheat oven to 350°F.

Place egg yolks, milk, flour and salt in blender or food processor container fitted with metal blade; process until smooth. Pour into bowl and let stand.

Melt butter in small skillet over medium heat. Add onion; cook until tender.

If using canned chiles, pat dry with paper towels. Slit each chili lengthwise and carefully remove seeds. Place 1 strip cheese and 1 tablespoon onion in each chili; reshape chiles to cover cheese. Place 2 chiles in each of 4 greased 1½-cup gratin dishes, or place in single layer in 13×9-inch baking dish.

Beat egg whites until soft peaks form; fold into yolk mixture. Dividing mixture evenly, pour over chiles in gratin dishes (or pour entire mixture over casserole).

Bake 20 to 25 minutes or until topping is puffed and knife inserted in center comes out clean. Broil 4 inches below heat 30 seconds or until topping is golden brown. Serve with condiments.   *Makes 4 servings*

Tidbit

Chiles rellenos literally means "stuffed peppers." The traditional Mexican version is made of fresh mild green chiles that have been stuffed with cheese, coated with egg batter and then fried until crisp.

Spinach Sensation

½ **pound bacon slices**
1 **cup (8 ounces) sour cream**
3 **eggs, separated**
2 **tablespoons all-purpose flour**
⅛ **teaspoon black pepper**
1 **package (10 ounces) frozen**
   chopped spinach, thawed
   and squeezed dry
½ **cup (2 ounces) shredded**
   sharp Cheddar cheese
½ **cup dry bread crumbs**
1 **tablespoon margarine or**
   butter, melted

Preheat oven to 350°F. Spray
2-quart round baking dish with
nonstick cooking spray.

Place bacon in single layer in
large skillet; cook over medium
heat until crisp. Remove from
skillet; drain on paper towels.
Crumble and set aside.

Combine sour cream, egg yolks,
flour and pepper in large bowl; set
aside. Beat egg whites in medium
bowl with electric mixer at high
speed until stiff peaks form. Stir
¼ of egg whites into sour cream
mixture; fold in remaining egg
whites.

Arrange half of spinach in
prepared dish. Top with half of
sour cream mixture. Sprinkle
¼ cup cheese over sour cream
mixture. Sprinkle bacon over
cheese. Repeat layers, ending with
remaining ¼ cup cheese.

Combine bread crumbs and
margarine in small bowl; sprinkle
evenly over cheese.

Bake, uncovered, 30 to 35 minutes
or until egg mixture is set. Let
stand 5 minutes before serving.
Makes 6 servings

Tidbit

*Extra water from
thawed spinach can
affect the outcome of
your dish. To remove
excess moisture, put spinach
between a double layer of
paper towels and press until
spinach is dry.*

Spinach Sensation

Pizza for Breakfast

1 (6½-ounce) package pizza
    crust mix
1 pound BOB EVANS® Original
    Recipe Roll Sausage
1 cup diced fresh or drained
    canned tomatoes
8 ounces fresh mushrooms,
    sliced
1½ cups (6 ounces) shredded
    mozzarella cheese, divided
1½ cups (6 ounces) shredded
    sharp Cheddar cheese,
    divided
4 eggs
    Salt and pepper to taste
    Salsa (optional)

Preheat oven to 350°F. Prepare
crust mix according to package
directions. Spread pizza dough
into greased 13×9-inch baking
dish, making sure dough evenly
covers bottom and 2 inches up
sides of dish. Crumble and cook
sausage in medium skillet until
browned; drain well. Top crust
with sausage, tomatoes,
mushrooms, 1 cup mozzarella
cheese and 1 cup Cheddar cheese.
Bake 8 to 10 minutes or until crust
is golden brown at edges. Remove
from oven. Whisk eggs, salt and
pepper in small bowl; pour over
pizza. Return to oven; bake 7 to
9 minutes more or until eggs are
set. Immediately sprinkle with
remaining cheeses. Serve hot, with
salsa, if desired. Refrigerate
leftovers.

Makes 8 to 10 servings

Ham 'n Egg Special Strata

¼ cup butter
2 cups sliced fresh mushrooms
1 medium onion, finely
    chopped
2 cups diced cooked ham
8 slices white bread, cubed
4 eggs
2½ cups milk
2 cups (8 ounces) shredded
    cheddar cheese
1 tablespoon prepared mustard
1 teaspoon LAWRY'S®
    Seasoned Salt
    Dash LAWRY'S® Seasoned
    Pepper

In medium skillet, heat butter. Add
mushrooms and onion and cook
over medium-high heat until tender;
stir in ham. In 13×9×2-inch baking
dish, place bread cubes; arrange
ham mixture over bread. In
medium bowl, combine remaining
ingredients; mix well. Pour over
bread cubes, making sure all are
moistened. Cover; refrigerate
overnight. Bake, uncovered, in
325°F oven 55 to 60 minutes.
Serve immediately.

Makes 6 to 8 servings

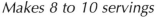

Pizza for Breakfast

Make It Meaty

pg. 178

pg. 186

Pork Chops and Stuffing Bake

6 (¾-inch-thick) boneless pork
   loin chops (about
   1½ pounds)
¼ teaspoon salt
⅛ teaspoon black pepper
1 tablespoon vegetable oil
1 small onion, chopped
2 ribs celery, chopped
2 Granny Smith apples, peeled,
   cored and coarsely
   chopped (about 2 cups)
1 can (14½ ounces) reduced-
   sodium chicken broth
1 can (10¾ ounces) condensed
   cream of celery soup,
   undiluted
¼ cup dry white wine
6 cups herb-seasoned stuffing
   cubes

Preheat oven to 375°F. Spray
13×9-inch baking dish with
nonstick cooking spray.

Season both sides of pork chops
with salt and pepper. Heat oil in
large deep skillet over medium-high
heat until hot. Add chops; cook
until browned on both sides,
turning once. Remove chops from
skillet; set aside.

Add onion and celery to same
skillet. Cook and stir 3 minutes or
until onion is tender. Add apples;
cook and stir 1 minute. Add broth,
soup and wine; mix well. Bring to

continued on page 176

Pork Chop and Stuffing Bake

Pork Chops and Stuffing Bake,
continued

a simmer; remove from heat. Stir in stuffing cubes until evenly moistened.

Pour stuffing mixture into prepared dish, spreading evenly. Place pork chops on top of stuffing; pour any accumulated juices over chops.

Cover tightly with foil and bake 30 to 40 minutes or until pork chops are juicy and barely pink in center.   *Makes 6 servings*

Easy Beef Lasagna

- **1 pound ground beef**
- **1 jar (26 to 28 ounces) RAGÚ® Old World Style® Pasta Sauce**
- **1 container (15 ounces) ricotta cheese**
- **2 cups shredded mozzarella cheese (about 8 ounces)**
- **½ cup grated Parmesan cheese, divided**
- **2 eggs**
- **12 lasagna noodles, cooked and drained**

1. Preheat oven to 375°F. In 12-inch skillet, brown ground beef; drain. Stir in Ragú Pasta Sauce; heat through.

2. In large bowl, combine ricotta cheese, mozzarella cheese, ¼ cup Parmesan cheese and eggs.

3. In 13×9-inch baking dish, evenly spread 1 cup meat sauce. Arrange 4 lasagna noodles lengthwise over sauce, then 1 cup meat sauce and ½ of the ricotta cheese mixture; repeat, ending with sauce. Cover with aluminum foil and bake 30 minutes. Bake uncovered an additional 5 minutes. Let stand 10 minutes before serving.
           Makes 10 servings

Prep Time: 30 minutes
Cook Time: 35 minutes

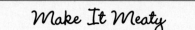
Cheesy Ham Casserole

2 cups fresh or frozen broccoli flowerets, thawed
1½ cups KRAFT® Shredded Sharp Cheddar Cheese, divided
1½ cups coarsely chopped ham
1½ cups (4 ounces) corkscrew pasta, cooked, drained
½ cup MIRACLE WHIP® or MIRACLE WHIP® LIGHT® Dressing
½ green or red bell pepper, chopped
¼ cup milk
Seasoned croutons (optional)

● Heat oven to 350°F.

● Mix all ingredients except ½ cup cheese and croutons.

● Spoon into 1½-quart casserole. Sprinkle with remaining ½ cup cheese.

● Bake 30 minutes or until thoroughly heated. Sprinkle with croutons, if desired.

Makes 4 to 6 servings

Prep Time: 15 minutes
Cook Time: 30 minutes

Santa Fe Casserole Bake

1 pound ground beef
1 package (1.0 ounce) LAWRY'S® Taco Spices & Seasonings
2 cups chicken broth
¼ cup all-purpose flour
1 cup dairy sour cream
1 can (7 ounces) diced green chilies
1 package (11 ounces) corn or tortilla chips
2 cups (8 ounces) shredded Monterey Jack or cheddar cheese
½ cup sliced green onions with tops

In medium skillet, cook ground beef until browned and crumbly; drain fat. Add Taco Spices & Seasonings; mix well. In small saucepan, combine broth and flour; bring to a boil over medium-high heat to slightly thicken liquid. Stir in sour cream and chilies; mix well. In 13×9×2-inch lightly greased glass baking dish, place ½ of chips. Top with ½ of beef mixture, ½ of sauce, ½ of cheese and ½ of green onions. Layer again with remaining ingredients, ending with green onions. Bake, uncovered, in 375°F oven 20 minutes. Let stand 5 minutes before cutting.

Makes 6 servings

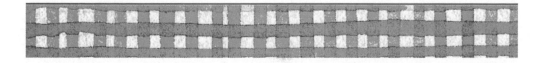

Tuscan Pot Pie

¾ **pound sweet or hot Italian
    sausage**
1 **jar (26 to 28 ounces)
    prepared chunky vegetable
    or mushroom spaghetti
    sauce**
1 **can (19 ounces) cannellini
    beans, rinsed and drained**
½ **teaspoon dried thyme leaves**
1½ **cups (6 ounces) shredded
    mozzarella cheese**
1 **package (8 ounces)
    refrigerated crescent
    dinner rolls**

1. Preheat oven to 425°F. Remove
sausage from casings. Brown
sausage in medium ovenproof
skillet, stirring to separate meat.
Drain drippings.

2. Add spaghetti sauce, beans and
thyme to skillet. Simmer, uncovered,
over medium heat 5 minutes.
Remove from heat; stir in cheese.

3. Unroll crescent dough; divide
into triangles. Arrange spiral-
fashion with points of dough
towards center, covering sausage
mixture completely. Bake
12 minutes or until crust is golden
brown and meat mixture is bubbly.
Makes 4 to 6 servings

Prep and Cook Time: 27 minutes

Pork Chops and Yams

4 **pork chops (½ inch thick)**
2 **tablespoons oil**
2 **(16-ounce) cans yams or
    sweet potatoes, drained**
¾ **cup SMUCKER'S® Sweet
    Orange Marmalade or
    Apricot Preserves**
½ **large green bell pepper, cut
    into strips**
2 **tablespoons minced onion**

Brown pork chops in oil over
medium heat.

Place yams in 1½-quart casserole.
Stir in marmalade, bell pepper and
onion. Layer pork chops over yam
mixture. Cover and bake at 350°F
for 30 minutes or until pork chops
are tender.　　*Makes 4 servings*

Tidbit

To remove a sausage
casing, use a paring
knife to slit the casing
at one end. Be careful
not to cut through the sausage.
Grasp the cut edge and gently
pull the casing away from the
sausage.

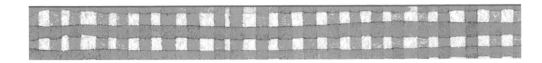

Tuscan Pot Pie

Stuffed Bell Peppers

3 large bell peppers, any color, seeded and cut in half lengthwise
1½ cups chopped fresh tomatoes
1 tablespoon chopped fresh cilantro
1 jalapeño pepper,* seeded and chopped
1 clove garlic, finely minced
½ teaspoon dried oregano leaves, divided
¼ teaspoon ground cumin
8 ounces lean ground round
1 cup cooked brown rice
¼ cup cholesterol-free egg substitute *or* 2 egg whites
2 tablespoons finely chopped onion
¼ teaspoon salt
⅛ teaspoon black pepper

*Jalapeño peppers can sting and irritate the skin; wear rubber gloves when handling peppers and do not touch eyes. Wash hands after handling.

1. Preheat oven to 350°F.

2. Place steamer basket in large saucepan; add 1 inch of water, being careful not to let water touch bottom of basket. Place bell peppers in basket; cover. Bring to a boil; reduce heat to medium. Steam peppers 8 to 10 minutes or until tender, adding additional water if necessary; drain.

3. Combine tomatoes, cilantro, jalapeño pepper, garlic, ¼ teaspoon oregano and cumin in small bowl; set aside.

4. Thoroughly combine beef, rice, egg substitute, onion, salt and black pepper in large bowl. Stir 1 cup of tomato mixture into beef mixture. Spoon filling evenly into pepper halves; place in 13×9-inch baking dish. Cover tightly with foil.

5. Bake 45 minutes or until meat is browned and vegetables are tender. Serve with remaining tomato salsa, if desired.

Makes 6 servings

Tidbit

Keep skins of stuffed peppers supple by rubbing a little oil on the outsides of the peppers before baking.

Stuffed Bell Peppers

Pizza Pasta

1 tablespoon vegetable oil
1 medium green bell pepper, chopped
1 medium onion, chopped
1 cup sliced mushrooms
½ teaspoon LAWRY'S® Garlic Powder with Parsley OR Garlic Salt
¼ cup sliced ripe olives
1 package (1.5 ounces) LAWRY'S® Original-Style Spaghetti Sauce Spices & Seasonings
1¾ cups water
1 can (6 ounces) tomato paste
10 ounces mostaccioli, cooked and drained
3 ounces thinly sliced pepperoni
¾ cup shredded mozzarella cheese

In large skillet, heat vegetable oil; add bell pepper, onion, mushrooms and Garlic Powder with Parsley and cook over medium-high heat. Stir in olives, Spaghetti Sauce Spices & Seasonings, water and tomato paste; mix well. Bring sauce to a boil over medium-high heat; reduce heat to low and simmer, uncovered, 10 minutes. Add cooked mostaccioli and sliced pepperoni; mix well. Pour into 12×8×2-inch baking dish; top with cheese. Bake at 350°F 15 minutes until cheese is melted.

Makes 6 servings

Hunter's Pie

2 tablespoons salad oil
6 loin-cut lamb chops, cut into bite-size pieces
 LAWRY'S® Seasoned Salt to taste
 LAWRY'S® Seasoned Pepper to taste
4 cups mashed potatoes
¼ cup butter, melted
¼ teaspoon white pepper
1 side of 1 Twin Pack (1.95 ounces) LAWRY'S® Brown Gravy
1 cup water

In large skillet, heat oil and add lamb, Seasoned Salt and Seasoned Pepper; brown. Drain fat. In medium bowl, combine potatoes, butter and white pepper; blend well. Butter shallow casserole dish and line with half of potato mixture. Top with lamb. Spread remaining potatoes over top. Bake, uncovered, in 350°F oven 45 minutes. Meanwhile, in medium saucepan, prepare Brown Gravy with water according to package directions. Cut a hole in top of potato crust; pour about half of gravy into pie.

Makes 6 servings

Serving Suggestion: Pass remaining gravy at the table.

Hint: Use 1½ pounds cubed lamb or ground lamb, formed into meatballs, in place of loin chops.

Lamb & Pork Cassoulet

1 package (1 pound) dry white navy beans, rinsed
Water
½ pound salt pork, sliced
1½ pounds boneless lamb shoulder or leg, cut into 1-inch cubes
4 large pork chops
½ pound pork sausages
Salt
Pepper
2 large onions, chopped
1 can (28 ounces) tomatoes, drained
½ cup dry red wine
3 cloves garlic, finely chopped
¼ cup chopped fresh parsley
1 teaspoon dried thyme, crushed
1 bay leaf

Place beans in large bowl. Cover with cold water; soak overnight. Drain and rinse beans. Place beans in Dutch oven; cover with cold water. Bring to a boil over high heat, skimming foam as necessary. Reduce heat to low. Cover and simmer about 1 hour. Drain beans, reserving liquid.

Cook salt pork in large skillet over medium-high heat until some of the fat is rendered. Remove salt pork. In batches, brown lamb, pork chops and sausages in fat. Remove from skillet; drain on paper towels. Cut chops and sausages into 1-inch pieces.

Sprinkle meat with salt and pepper. Remove all but 2 tablespoons of the fat from skillet. Add onions. Cook and stir over medium-high heat until onions are tender. Add tomatoes, wine, garlic, parsley, thyme and bay leaf. Combine tomato mixture, drained beans and meats in large bowl. Spoon into large casserole. Pour reserved bean liquid over mixture just to cover. Bake at 350°F about 1½ hours or until meat is fork-tender. Remove bay leaf before serving.

Makes 6 to 8 servings

Favorite recipe from **American Lamb Council**

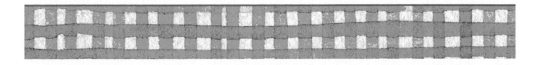

Southwestern-Style Beef Stew

¼ cup all-purpose flour
1 teaspoon seasoned salt
¼ teaspoon ground black pepper
2 pounds beef stew meat, cut into bite-size pieces
2 tablespoons vegetable oil
1 large onion, cut into wedges
2 large cloves garlic, finely chopped
1¾ cups (14½-ounce can) stewed tomatoes, undrained
1¾ cups (16-ounce jar) ORTEGA® Garden Style Salsa, mild
1 cup beef broth
1 tablespoon ground oregano
1 teaspoon ground cumin
½ teaspoon salt
3 large carrots, peeled, cut into 1-inch slices
1¾ cups (15-ounce can) garbanzo beans, drained
1 cup (8-ounce can) baby corn, drained, halved

COMBINE flour, salt and pepper in medium bowl or large resealable plastic food-storage bag. Add meat; toss well to coat.

HEAT oil in large saucepan over medium-high heat. Add meat, onion and garlic; cook for 5 to 6 minutes or until meat is browned on outside and onion is tender. Stir in tomatoes with juice, salsa, broth, oregano, cumin and salt. Bring to a boil; cover. Reduce heat to low; cook, stirring occasionally, for 45 minutes or until meat is tender.

STIR in carrots, beans and baby corn. Increase heat to medium-low. Cook, stirring occasionally, for 30 to 40 minutes or until carrots are tender.

Makes 8 servings

Tidbit

Garbanzo beans are also called chick-peas. These pale yellow legumes are somewhat round, but have irregularly shaped surfaces. They are used in many Mediterranean, Middle Eastern and Indian dishes.

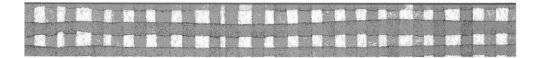

Southwestern-Style Beef Stew

Biscuit-Topped Hearty Steak Pie

1½ pounds top round steak, cooked and cut into 1-inch cubes
1 package (9 ounces) frozen baby carrots
1 package (9 ounces) frozen peas and pearl onions
1 large baking potato, cooked and cut into ½-inch pieces
1 jar (18 ounces) home-style brown gravy
½ teaspoon dried thyme leaves
½ teaspoon black pepper
1 can (10 ounces) refrigerated flaky buttermilk biscuits

Preheat oven to 375°F. Spray 2-quart casserole with nonstick cooking spray.

Combine steak, frozen vegetables and potato in prepared dish. Stir in gravy, thyme and pepper.

Bake, uncovered, 40 minutes. Remove from oven. *Increase oven temperature to 400°F.* Top with biscuits and bake 8 to 10 minutes or until biscuits are golden brown.

Makes 6 servings

Note: This casserole can be prepared with leftovers of almost any kind. Other steaks, roast beef, stew meat, pork, lamb or chicken can be substituted for round steak; adjust gravy flavor to complement meat.

Fix-It-Fast Corned Beef & Cabbage

1 small head cabbage (about 1½ pounds), cored and cut into 6 wedges
1 can (12 ounces) corned beef, sliced, *or* ½ pound sliced deli corned beef
1 can (14 ounces) sliced carrots, drained
1 can (16 ounces) sliced potatoes, drained
1⅓ cups *French's*® *Taste Toppers*™ French Fried Onions, divided
1 can (10¾ ounces) condensed cream of celery soup
¾ cup water

Preheat oven to 375°F. Arrange cabbage wedges and corned beef slices alternately down center of 13×9-inch baking dish. Place carrots, potatoes and ⅔ *cup **Taste Toppers*** along sides of dish. In small bowl, combine soup and water; pour over meat and vegetables. Bake, covered, at 375°F for 40 minutes or until cabbage is tender. Top with remaining ⅔ *cup **Taste Toppers***; bake, uncovered, 3 minutes or until ***Taste Toppers*** are golden brown. *Makes 4 to 6 servings*

Biscuit-Topped Hearty Steak Pie

Potluck Poultry

pg. 192

pg. 202

Chicken Enchiladas

2 cups chopped cooked chicken
   or turkey
1 cup chopped green bell
   pepper
1 package (8 ounces)
   PHILADELPHIA® Cream
   Cheese, cubed
1 jar (8 ounces) salsa, divided
8 (6-inch) flour tortillas
¾ pound (12 ounces)
   VELVEETA® Pasteurized
   Process Cheese Spread,
   cut up
¼ cup milk

STIR chicken, bell pepper, cream cheese and ½ cup salsa in saucepan on low heat until cream cheese is melted.

SPOON ⅓ cup chicken mixture down center of each tortilla; roll up. Place, seam-side down, in lightly greased 12×8-inch baking dish.

STIR process cheese spread and milk in saucepan on low heat until smooth. Pour sauce over tortillas; cover with foil.

BAKE at 350°F for 20 minutes or until thoroughly heated. Pour remaining salsa over tortillas.
Makes 4 to 6 servings

Prep Time: 20 minutes
Bake Time: 20 minutes

Chicken Enchiladas

Spicy Turkey Casserole

1 tablespoon olive oil
1 pound turkey breast cutlets, cut into ½-inch pieces
2 (3-ounce) spicy chicken or turkey sausages, sliced ½ inch thick
1 cup diced green bell pepper
½ cup sliced mushrooms
½ cup diced onion
1 jalapeño pepper,* seeded and minced (optional)
½ cup fat-free reduced-sodium chicken broth or water
1 can (14 ounces) reduced-sodium diced tomatoes, undrained
1 teaspoon Italian seasoning
½ teaspoon paprika
¼ teaspoon black pepper
1 cup cooked egg yolk-free egg noodles
6 tablespoons grated Parmesan cheese
2 tablespoons coarse bread crumbs

*Jalapeño peppers can sting and irritate the skin; wear rubber gloves when handling peppers and do not touch eyes. Wash hands after handling.

1. Preheat oven to 350°F. Heat oil in large nonstick skillet. Add turkey and sausages; cook and stir over medium heat 2 minutes. Add bell pepper, mushrooms, onion and jalapeño pepper, if desired. Cook and stir 5 minutes. Add chicken broth; cook 1 minute, scraping any browned bits off bottom of skillet. Add tomatoes and liquid, seasonings and noodles.

2. Spoon turkey mixture into shallow 10-inch round casserole. Sprinkle with cheese and bread crumbs. Bake 15 to 20 minutes or until mixture is hot and bread crumbs are brown.

Makes 6 (1-cup) servings

Bayou Chicken Bake

4 to 6 PERDUE® Individually Frozen™ boneless, skinless chicken breasts
1½ to 2 teaspoons Cajun or Creole seasoning
½ cup chopped onion
1 cup uncooked regular long-grain rice
1 package (16 ounces) frozen black-eyed peas
2 cans (14½ ounces each) Cajun-style stewed tomatoes
2 tablespoons chopped fresh parsley

Preheat oven to 350°F. Lightly grease 13×9-inch baking dish. Sprinkle chicken with Cajun seasoning; place in baking dish. In large bowl, combine onion, rice, black-eyed peas and tomatoes. Pour over chicken. Cover and bake 45 minutes. Uncover and bake 15 minutes longer, or until chicken is cooked through. Sprinkle with parsley before serving.

Makes 4 to 6 servings

Spicy Turkey Casserole

Chicken Marsala

4 cups (6 ounces) uncooked
    broad egg noodles
½ cup Italian-style dry bread
    crumbs
1 teaspoon dried basil leaves
1 egg
1 teaspoon water
4 boneless skinless chicken
    breast halves
3 tablespoons olive oil, divided
¾ cup chopped onion
8 ounces cremini or button
    mushrooms, sliced
3 cloves garlic, minced
3 tablespoons all-purpose flour
1 can (14½ ounces) chicken
    broth
½ cup dry marsala wine
¾ teaspoon salt
¼ teaspoon black pepper
    Chopped fresh parsley
    (optional)

PREHEAT oven to 375°F. Spray 11×7-inch baking dish with nonstick cooking spray.

COOK noodles according to package directions until al dente. Drain and place in prepared dish.

Meanwhile, **COMBINE** bread crumbs and basil on shallow plate or pie plate. Beat egg with water on another shallow plate or pie plate. Dip chicken in egg mixture, letting excess drip off. Roll in crumb mixture, patting to coat.

HEAT 2 tablespoons oil in large skillet over medium-high heat until hot. Cook chicken 3 minutes per side or until browned. Transfer to clean plate; set aside.

HEAT remaining 1 tablespoon oil in same skillet over medium heat. Add onion; cook and stir 5 minutes. Add mushrooms and garlic; cook and stir 3 minutes. Sprinkle onion mixture with flour; cook and stir 1 minute. Add broth, wine, salt and pepper; bring to a boil over high heat. Cook and stir 5 minutes or until sauce thickens.

RESERVE ½ cup sauce. Pour remaining sauce over cooked noodles; stir until noodles are well coated. Place chicken on top of noodles. Spoon reserved sauce over chicken.

BAKE, uncovered, about 20 minutes or until chicken is no longer pink in center and sauce is hot and bubbly. Sprinkle with parsley, if desired.   *Makes 4 servings*

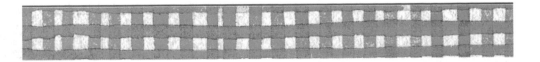

Chicken Marsala

Chicken & Biscuits

¼ cup butter or margarine
4 boneless skinless chicken
  breast halves (about
  1¼ pounds), cut into
  ½-inch pieces
½ cup chopped onion
½ teaspoon dried thyme leaves
½ teaspoon paprika
¼ teaspoon black pepper
1 can (about 14 ounces)
  chicken broth, divided
⅓ cup all-purpose flour
1 package (10 ounces) frozen
  peas and carrots
1 can (12 ounces) refrigerated
  biscuits

Preheat oven to 375°F. Melt butter in large skillet over medium heat. Add chicken, onion, thyme, paprika and pepper. Cook 5 minutes or until chicken is browned.

Combine ¼ cup chicken broth with flour; stir until smooth. Set aside.

Add remaining chicken broth to skillet; bring to a boil. Gradually add flour mixture, stirring constantly to prevent lumps from forming. Simmer 5 minutes. Add peas and carrots; continue cooking 2 minutes.

Transfer to 1½-quart casserole; top with biscuits. Bake 25 to 30 minutes or until biscuits are golden brown.
Makes 4 to 6 servings

Fettuccine with Chicken Breasts

12 ounces uncooked fettuccine
  or egg noodles
1 cup HIDDEN VALLEY®
  Original Ranch® Dressing
⅓ cup Dijon mustard
8 boneless, skinless chicken
  breast halves, pounded
  thin
½ cup butter
⅓ cup dry white wine

Cook fettuccine according to package directions; drain. Preheat oven to 425°F. Stir together dressing and mustard; set aside. Pour fettuccine into oiled baking dish. Sauté chicken in butter in a large skillet until no longer pink in center. Transfer cooked chicken to the bed of fettuccine. Add wine to the skillet; cook until reduced to desired consistency. Drizzle over chicken. Pour the reserved dressing mixture over the chicken. Bake at 425°F about 10 minutes, or until dressing forms a golden brown crust.
Makes 8 servings

Chicken & Biscuits

Creamy Chicken and Pasta with Spinach

6 ounces uncooked egg noodles
1 tablespoon olive oil
¼ cup chopped onion
¼ cup chopped red bell pepper
1 package (10 ounces) frozen spinach, thawed and drained
2 boneless skinless chicken breast halves (¾ pound), cooked and cut into 1-inch pieces
1 can (4 ounces) sliced mushrooms, drained
2 cups (8 ounces) shredded Swiss cheese
1 container (8 ounces) sour cream
¾ cup half-and-half
2 eggs, slightly beaten
½ teaspoon salt
Red onion and fresh spinach for garnish

Preheat oven to 350°F. Prepare egg noodles according to package directions; set aside.

Heat oil in large skillet over medium-high heat. Add onion and bell pepper; cook and stir 2 minutes or until onion is tender. Add spinach, chicken, mushrooms and cooked noodles; stir to combine.

Combine cheese, sour cream, half-and-half, eggs and salt in medium bowl; blend well.

Add cheese mixture to chicken mixture; stir to combine. Pour into 13×9-inch baking dish coated with nonstick cooking spray. Bake, covered, 30 to 35 minutes or until heated through. Garnish with red onion and fresh spinach, if desired.

Makes 8 servings

Brown Rice Chicken Bake

3 cups cooked brown rice
1 package (10 ounces) frozen green peas
2 cups chopped cooked chicken breasts
½ cup cholesterol free, reduced calorie mayonnaise
⅓ cup slivered almonds, toasted (optional)
2 teaspoons soy sauce
¼ teaspoon ground black pepper
¼ teaspoon garlic powder
¼ teaspoon dried tarragon leaves
Vegetable cooking spray

Spray 3-quart baking casserole with cooking spray. Combine rice, peas, chicken, mayonnaise, almonds, soy sauce, and seasonings in large bowl; mix well. Spoon into prepared casserole; cover. Bake at 350°F. for 15 to 20 minutes or until heated through.　　*Makes 6 servings*

Favorite recipe from **USA Rice Federation**

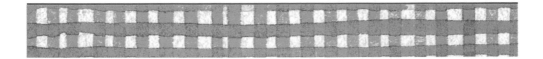

Turkey Manicotti

1 pound Italian turkey sausage
¼ pound fresh mushrooms, chopped
½ cup onion, chopped
1 clove garlic, minced
1½ cups low-fat ricotta cheese
1 cup (4 ounces) part-skim mozzarella cheese, grated
1 egg, beaten
1 package (10 ounces) frozen chopped spinach, defrosted and well drained
1 package (8 ounces) manicotti shells, cooked according to package directions and drained
Vegetable cooking spray
¼ cup flour
⅛ teaspoon pepper
1 can (15 ounces) evaporated skim milk
½ cup low-sodium chicken broth
½ cup plus 2 tablespoons Parmesan cheese

1. In large non-stick skillet, over medium heat, sauté turkey sausage, mushrooms, onion and garlic 5 to 6 minutes or until sausage is no longer pink. Remove skillet from heat and drain.

2. In large bowl combine ricotta cheese, mozzarella cheese and egg. Combine with turkey sausage mixture and spinach.

3. Cut each manicotti shell open down long side. This will make stuffing shells easier. Carefully spoon ⅓ cup turkey sausage filling down center of each shell. Roll up shell to encase turkey filling. Arrange stuffed shells, seam-side-down, on (11×14-inch) baking dish lightly coated with vegetable spray.

4. In medium saucepan combine flour and pepper. With wire whisk slowly combine evaporated milk and chicken broth with flour and pepper. Over medium heat, stirring constantly, heat sauce until it begins to boil and thickens. Remove pan from heat; whisk in ½ cup Parmesan cheese. Pour sauce over stuffed shells; sprinkle with remaining Parmesan cheese.

5. Cover baking pan with foil. Bake in 350°F oven 20 to 25 minutes or until mixture is heated through.

Makes 8 servings

Favorite recipe from **National Turkey Federation**

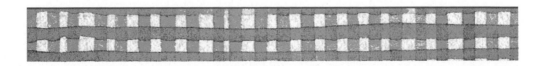

Spinach Quiche

1 medium leek
 Water
¼ cup butter or margarine
2 cups finely chopped cooked
   chicken
½ package (10 ounces) frozen
   chopped spinach or
   broccoli, cooked and
   drained
1 unbaked ready-to-use pie
   crust (10 inches in
   diameter)
1 tablespoon all-purpose flour
1½ cups (6 ounces) shredded
   Swiss cheese
1½ cups half-and-half or
   evaporated milk
4 eggs
2 tablespoons brandy
½ teaspoon salt
¼ teaspoon black pepper
¼ teaspoon ground nutmeg

Preheat oven to 375°F. Cut leek
in half lengthwise; wash and trim,
leaving 2 to 3 inches of green tops
intact. Cut leek halves crosswise
into thin slices. Place in small
saucepan; add enough water to
cover. Bring to a boil over high
heat; reduce heat and simmer
5 minutes. Drain; reserve leek.

Melt butter in large skillet over
medium heat. Add chicken; cook
until chicken is golden, about
5 minutes. Add spinach and leek
to chicken mixture; cook 1 to
2 minutes longer. Remove from
heat.

Spoon chicken mixture into pie
crust. Sprinkle flour and cheese
over chicken mixture. Combine
half-and-half, eggs, brandy, salt,
pepper and nutmeg in medium
bowl. Pour egg mixture over
cheese.

Bake 35 to 40 minutes or until
knife inserted into center comes
out clean. Let stand 5 minutes
before serving. Serve hot or cold.
Makes 6 servings

Tidbit

*A leek looks like an
oversized scallion. It
consists of long, flat,
dark green leaves on
top, and a white tubular
base. Its root end is
bulbous–similar to that
of a scallion.*

Spinach Quiche

Broccoli Cheese Casserole

3 whole chicken breasts, skinned and halved
1½ pounds fresh broccoli
2 tablespoons margarine
½ cup chopped onion
1 clove garlic, minced
3 tablespoons all-purpose flour
1¼ cups skim milk
2 tablespoons fresh parsley
½ teaspoon salt
½ teaspoon dried oregano leaves, crushed
1½ cups 1% low fat cream-style small curd cottage cheese
1½ cups shredded reduced fat Wisconsin Cheddar cheese
¼ cup grated Wisconsin Romano cheese
1 jar (4½ ounces) sliced mushrooms, drained
6 ounces noodles, cooked and drained

MICROWAVE DIRECTIONS:
Place chicken breasts in microwavable glass baking dish. Microwave at HIGH (100% power) 7 minutes. Cool slightly and cube. Set aside. Remove flowerets from broccoli and cut larger ones in half. Cut stems into 1-inch pieces. Place broccoli in 3-quart microwavable baking dish with ½ cup water. Cover and microwave at HIGH (100% power) 7 minutes, stirring once. Let stand, covered, 2 minutes. Drain well; set aside.

Place margarine, onion and garlic in same baking dish. Cover and microwave at HIGH (100% power) 3 minutes. Stir in flour. Gradually add milk. Add parsley, salt and oregano. Microwave at HIGH (100% power) 1 minute. Stir well; microwave 1 minute. Stir in cottage cheese. Microwave at HIGH (100% power) 2 minutes. Stir; microwave 2 minutes. Add Cheddar and Romano cheeses, stirring well. Microwave at MEDIUM-HIGH (70% power) 2 minutes. Stir in chicken, broccoli, mushrooms and noodles. Cover and microwave at MEDIUM (50% power) 5 minutes or until heated through.

Makes 6 to 8 servings

Favorite recipe from **Wisconsin Milk Marketing Board**

Trim Turkey Tetrazzini

½ pound BUTTERBALL® Oven Roasted Turkey Breast, sliced ½ inch thick in the deli, cubed
½ pound uncooked spaghetti, broken
¼ cup butter or margarine
¼ cup flour
1 can (14½ ounces) fat free reduced sodium chicken broth
2¾ cups milk
½ teaspoon salt
¼ teaspoon ground white pepper
8 ounces fresh mushrooms, sliced
¼ cup grated Parmesan cheese
½ cup crumbled salad croutons

Cook and drain spaghetti. Melt butter in large skillet over medium heat. Whisk in flour. Add chicken broth, milk, salt and pepper. Heat, stirring constantly, until thickened. Add turkey, mushrooms, Parmesan cheese and spaghetti to skillet. Spray 13×9-inch baking dish with nonstick cooking spray. Pour turkey mixture into baking dish. Top with crumbled croutons. Bake 30 to 40 minutes in preheated 350°F oven. *Makes 8 servings*

Preparation Time: 15 minutes plus baking time

Chilaquiles

1 can (10¾ ounces) condensed cream of chicken soup
½ cup mild green chili salsa
1 can (4 ounces) diced green chilies, undrained
8 cups taco chips
2 to 3 cups shredded cooked turkey or chicken
2 cups (8 ounces) shredded Cheddar cheese
Sliced pitted black olives for garnish
Cilantro sprigs for garnish

Preheat oven to 350°F. Combine soup and salsa in medium bowl; stir in green chilies. Place ⅓ of chips in 2- to 2½-quart casserole; top with ⅓ of turkey. Spread ⅓ of soup mixture over turkey; sprinkle with ⅓ of cheese. Repeat layering. Bake, uncovered, 15 minutes or until casserole is heated through and cheese is melted. Garnish with olives and cilantro.
Makes 6 servings

Turkey Vegetable Crescent Pie

2 cans (about 14 ounces)
    fat-free reduced-sodium
    chicken broth
1 medium onion, diced
1¼ pounds turkey tenderloins,
    cut into ¾-inch pieces
3 cups diced red potatoes
1 teaspoon chopped fresh
    rosemary *or* ½ teaspoon
    dried rosemary
¼ teaspoon salt
⅛ teaspoon black pepper
1 bag (16 ounces) frozen
    mixed vegetables
1 bag (10 ounces) frozen mixed
    vegetables
⅓ cup fat-free (skim) milk plus
    additional if necessary
3 tablespoons cornstarch
1 package (8 ounces)
    refrigerated reduced-fat
    crescent rolls

1. Bring broth to a boil in large saucepan. Add onion; reduce heat and simmer 3 minutes. Add turkey; return to a boil. Reduce heat; cover and simmer 7 to 9 minutes or until turkey is no longer pink. Remove turkey from saucepan with slotted spoon; place in 13×9-inch baking dish.

2. Return broth to a boil. Add potatoes, rosemary, salt and pepper; simmer 2 minutes. Return to a boil; stir in mixed vegetables. Simmer, covered, 7 to 8 minutes or until potatoes are tender.

Remove vegetables with slotted spoon. Drain in colander set over bowl; reserve broth. Transfer vegetables to baking dish with turkey.

3. Preheat oven to 375°F. Blend ⅓ cup milk with cornstarch in small bowl until smooth. Add enough milk to reserved broth to equal 3 cups. Heat in large saucepan over medium-high heat; whisk in cornstarch mixture, stirring constantly until mixture comes to a boil. Boil 1 minute; remove from heat. Pour over turkey-vegetable mixture in baking dish.

4. Roll out crescent roll dough; separate at perforations. Arrange dough pieces decoratively over top of turkey-vegetable mixture. Bake 13 to 15 minutes or until crust is golden brown.

Makes 8 servings

Turkey Vegetable Crescent Pie

Deep-Sea Dishes

Shrimp Primavera Pot Pie

1 can (10¾ ounces) condensed cream of shrimp soup, undiluted
1 package (12 ounces) frozen peeled uncooked medium shrimp
2 packages (1 pound each) frozen mixed vegetables, such as green beans, potatoes, onions and red peppers, thawed and drained
1 teaspoon dried dill weed
¼ teaspoon salt
¼ teaspoon black pepper
1 package (11 ounces) refrigerated soft breadstick dough

pg. 206

pg. 214

1. Preheat oven to 400°F. Heat soup in medium ovenproof skillet over medium-high heat 1 minute. Add shrimp; cook and stir 3 minutes or until shrimp begin to thaw. Stir in vegetables, dill, salt and pepper; mix well. Reduce heat to medium-low; cook and stir 3 minutes.

2. Unwrap breadstick dough; separate into 8 strips. Twist strips, cutting to fit skillet. Arrange attractively over shrimp mixture. Press ends of dough lightly to edges of skillet to secure. Bake 18 minutes or until crust is golden brown and shrimp mixture is bubbly.

Makes 4 to 6 servings

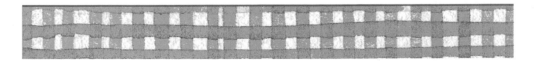

Shrimp Primavera Pot Pie

Tuna Pot Pie

- 1 tablespoon margarine or butter
- 1 small onion, chopped
- 1 can (10¾ ounces) condensed cream of potato soup, undiluted
- ¼ cup milk
- ½ teaspoon dried thyme leaves
- ¼ teaspoon salt
- ⅛ teaspoon black pepper
- 2 cans (6 ounces each) albacore tuna in water, drained
- 1 package (16 ounces) frozen vegetable medley (such as broccoli, green beans, carrots and red peppers), thawed
- 2 tablespoons chopped fresh parsley
- 1 can (8 ounces) refrigerated crescent roll dough

Preheat oven to 350°F. Spray 11×7-inch baking dish with nonstick cooking spray.

Melt margarine in large skillet over medium heat. Add onion; cook and stir 2 minutes or until onion is tender. Add soup, milk, thyme, salt and pepper; cook and stir 3 to 4 minutes or until thick and bubbly. Stir in tuna, vegetables and parsley. Pour mixture into prepared dish.

Unroll crescent roll dough and divide into triangles. Place triangles over tuna filling without overlapping dough.

Bake, uncovered, 20 minutes or until triangles are golden brown. Let stand 5 minutes before serving. Garnish as desired.

Makes 6 servings

Fillets Stuffed with Crabmeat

- 1 envelope LIPTON® RECIPE SECRETS® Savory Herb with Garlic Soup Mix*
- ½ cup fresh bread crumbs
- 1 package (6 ounces) frozen crabmeat, thawed and well-drained
- ½ cup water
- 2 teaspoons lemon juice
- 4 fish fillets (about 1 pound)
- 1 tablespoon margarine or butter, melted

*Also terrific with LIPTON® RECIPE SECRETS® Golden Onion Soup Mix.

Preheat oven to 350°F.

In medium bowl, combine savory herb with garlic soup mix, bread crumbs, crabmeat, water and lemon juice.

Top fillets evenly with crabmeat mixture; roll up and secure with wooden toothpicks. Place in lightly greased 2-quart oblong baking dish. Brush fish with margarine and bake 25 minutes or until fish flakes. Remove toothpicks before serving.

Makes 4 servings

Tuna Pot Pie

Jumbo Shells Seafood Fancies

1 package (16 ounces) uncooked jumbo pasta shells
1 can (7½ ounces) crabmeat
4 ounces (1 cup) grated Swiss cheese
1 can (2½ ounces) tiny shrimp, drained
½ cup mayonnaise
2 tablespoons thinly sliced celery
1 tablespoon chopped onion
1 tablespoon finely chopped pimiento

1. Cook shells according to package directions until tender but still firm; drain. Rinse under cold running water; drain again.

2. Invert shells onto paper towel-lined plate to drain and cool.

3. Drain and discard liquid from crabmeat. Place crabmeat in large bowl; flake with fork into small pieces. Remove any bits of shell or cartilage.

4. Add remaining ingredients to crabmeat. If mixture seems too dry, add more mayonnaise.

5. Using large spoon, stuff cooled shells with seafood mixture.

6. Cover; refrigerate until chilled. Garnish, if desired.

Makes 8 servings

Sole Almondine

1 package (6.5 ounces) RICE-A-RONI® Broccoli Au Gratin
1 medium zucchini
4 sole, scrod or orange roughy fillets
1 tablespoon lemon juice
¼ cup grated Parmesan cheese, divided
Salt and pepper (optional)
¼ cup sliced almonds
2 tablespoons margarine or butter, melted

1. Prepare Rice-A-Roni® Mix as package directs.

2. While Rice-A-Roni® is simmering, cut zucchini lengthwise into 12 thin slices. Heat oven to 350°F.

3. In 11×7-inch glass baking dish, spread prepared rice evenly. Set aside. Sprinkle fish with lemon juice, 2 tablespoons cheese, salt and pepper, if desired. Place zucchini strips over fish; roll up. Place fish seam-side down on rice.

4. Combine almonds and margarine; sprinkle evenly over fish. Top with remaining 2 tablespoons cheese. Bake 20 to 25 minutes or until fish flakes easily with fork.

Makes 4 servings

Tuna-Noodle Casserole

1 tablespoon butter
¾ cup diced onion
1 can cream of mushroom
    soup
1 cup milk
3 cups hot cooked egg noodles
2 cans tuna, drained and
    flaked
1¼ cups frozen peas
1 jar diced pimientos, drained
1 tablespoon lemon juice
¼ teaspoon salt
¼ teaspoon black pepper
½ cup fresh bread crumbs
½ cup grated BELGIOIOSO®
    Parmesan Cheese

Preheat oven to 450°F. Melt butter in medium saucepan over medium-high heat. Add onion; sauté 3 minutes. Add soup and milk. Cook 3 minutes, whisking constantly. Combine soup mixture, noodles, tuna, peas, pimientos, lemon juice, salt and pepper in 2-quart casserole. Combine bread crumbs and BelGioioso Parmesan Cheese in separate bowl; sprinkle on top of tuna mixture. Bake at 450°F for 15 minutes or until bubbly.   *Makes 4 servings*

Shrimp Casserole

¾ pound raw medium Florida
    shrimp, peeled, deveined
⅓ cup chopped celery
¼ cup chopped onion
¼ cup chopped green bell
    pepper
3 tablespoons margarine
1 can (10¾ ounces) condensed
    cream of celery soup
½ cup dry stuffing mix
1 hard-boiled egg, chopped
⅓ cup sliced water chestnuts
1 tablespoon lemon juice
¼ teaspoon salt
¼ cup (1 ounce) shredded
    Cheddar cheese

MICROWAVE DIRECTIONS

Halve large shrimp. In 1½-quart shallow casserole, combine shrimp, celery, onion, bell pepper and margarine. Cover; cook on HIGH 4 minutes, stirring after 2 minutes. Stir in soup, stuffing mix, egg, water chestnuts, juice and salt. Cover; cook on HIGH 4 minutes. Sprinkle with cheese; cook, uncovered, on HIGH 1 minute.   *Makes 4 servings*

Favorite recipe from *Florida Department of Agriculture and Consumer Services, Bureau of Seafood and Aquaculture*

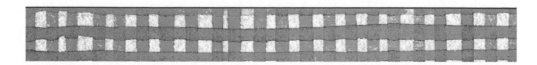

Pasta with Salmon and Dill

6 ounces uncooked mafalda
   pasta
1 tablespoon olive oil
2 ribs celery, sliced
1 small red onion, chopped
1 can (10¾ ounces) condensed
   cream of celery soup
¼ cup reduced-fat mayonnaise
¼ cup dry white wine
3 tablespoons chopped fresh
   parsley
1 teaspoon dried dill weed
1 can (7½ ounces) pink
   salmon, drained
½ cup dry bread crumbs
1 tablespoon margarine or
   butter, melted
   Fresh dill sprigs (optional)
   Red onion slices (optional)

Preheat oven to 350°F. Spray
1-quart square baking dish with
nonstick cooking spray.

Cook pasta according to package
directions until al dente; drain and
set aside.

Meanwhile, heat oil in medium
skillet over medium-high heat
until hot. Add celery and onion;
cook and stir 2 minutes or until
vegetables are tender. Set aside.

Combine soup, mayonnaise, wine,
parsley and dill weed in large bowl.
Stir in pasta, vegetables and salmon
until pasta is well coated. Pour
salmon mixture into prepared dish.

Combine bread crumbs and
margarine in small bowl; sprinkle
evenly over casserole. Bake,
uncovered, 25 minutes or until hot
and bubbly. Garnish with dill
sprigs and onion slices, if desired.
Makes 4 servings

Seafood Quiche

1 package (8 ounces)
   PHILADELPHIA® Cream
   Cheese, softened
1 can (6 ounces) crabmeat,
   drained, flaked
4 eggs
½ cup sliced green onions
½ cup milk
½ teaspoon dill weed
½ teaspoon lemon and pepper
   seasoning salt
1 (9-inch) baked pastry shell

MIX all ingredients except pastry
shell with electric mixer on
medium speed until well blended.

POUR into pastry shell.

BAKE at 350°F for 40 minutes or
until knife inserted in center comes
out clean. Let stand 10 minutes
before serving.
Makes 6 to 8 servings

Prep Time: 15 minutes
Bake Time: 40 minutes plus
standing

Pasta with Salmon and Dill

Shrimp Noodle Supreme

1 package (8 ounces) spinach noodles, cooked and drained
1 package (3 ounces) cream cheese, cubed and softened
1½ pounds medium shrimp, peeled and deveined
½ cup butter, softened
  Salt
  Black pepper
1 can (10¾ ounces) condensed cream of mushroom soup
1 cup sour cream
½ cup half-and-half
½ cup mayonnaise
1 tablespoon snipped chives
1 tablespoon chopped fresh parsley
½ teaspoon Dijon mustard
¾ cup (6 ounces) shredded sharp Cheddar cheese

Preheat oven to 325°F. Combine noodles and cream cheese in medium bowl. Spread noodle mixture into bottom of greased 13×9-inch glass casserole. Cook shrimp in butter in large skillet over medium-high heat until pink and tender, about 5 minutes. Season to taste with salt and pepper. Spread shrimp over noodles.

Combine soup, sour cream, half-and-half, mayonnaise, chives, parsley and mustard in another medium bowl. Spread over shrimp.

Sprinkle Cheddar cheese over top. Bake 25 minutes or until hot and cheese is melted. Garnish, if desired. *Makes 6 servings*

Fish a la Paolo

1 (16-ounce) jar NEWMAN'S OWN® Medium Salsa
1 (10-ounce) package frozen chopped spinach, thawed, drained and squeezed dry (or favorite mild vegetable)
2 tablespoons capers
1 tablespoon lemon juice
1 pound firm fresh fish, such as scrod fillets, cut into 4 pieces
1 tablespoon butter, cut into small pieces
1 large tomato, thinly sliced
½ cup fresh cilantro leaves, chopped

Preheat oven to 400°F. Mix salsa with spinach, capers and lemon juice; place in bottom of 11×7-inch baking dish. Place fish on top. Dot fish with butter and top with tomato slices.

Bake 25 minutes. Remove from oven and top with chopped cilantro. *Makes 4 servings*

Shrimp Noodle Supreme

Paella

¼ cup FILIPPO BERIO® Olive Oil
1 pound boneless skinless chicken breasts, cut into 1-inch strips
½ pound Italian sausage, cut into 1-inch slices
1 onion, chopped
3 cloves garlic, minced
2 (14½-ounce) cans chicken broth
2 cups uncooked long grain white rice
1 (8-ounce) bottle clam juice
1 (2-ounce) jar chopped pimientos, drained
2 bay leaves
1 teaspoon salt
¼ teaspoon saffron threads, crumbled (optional)
1 pound raw shrimp, shelled and deveined
1 (16-ounce) can whole tomatoes, drained
1 (10-ounce) package frozen peas, thawed
12 littleneck clams, scrubbed
¼ cup water
    Fresh herb sprig (optional)

Preheat oven to 350°F. In large skillet, heat olive oil over medium heat until hot. Add chicken; cook and stir 8 to 10 minutes or until brown on all sides. Remove with slotted spoon; set aside. Add sausage to skillet; cook and stir 8 to 10 minutes or until brown. Remove with slotted spoon; set aside. Add onion and garlic to skillet; cook and stir 5 to 7 minutes or until onion is tender. Transfer chicken, sausage, onion and garlic mixture to large casserole.

Add chicken broth, rice, clam juice, pimiento, bay leaves, salt and saffron, if desired, to chicken mixture. Cover; bake 30 minutes. Add shrimp, tomatoes and peas; stir well. Cover; bake an additional 15 minutes or until rice is tender, liquid is absorbed and shrimp are opaque. Remove bay leaves.

Meanwhile, combine clams and water in stockpot or large saucepan. Cover; cook over medium heat 5 to 10 minutes or until clams open; remove clams immediately as they open. Discard any clams with unopened shells. Place clams on top of paella. Garnish with herb sprig, if desired.

Makes 4 to 6 servings

Tidbit

Make sure to only buy clams with tightly closed shells. If you find any of them are even slightly open, tap them lightly. Live clams will snap shut. Discard any that don't snap shut.

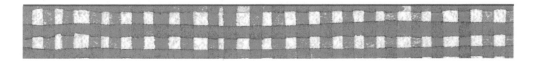

Paella

Meatless Meals

pg. 220

pg. 226

Three Cheese Baked Ziti

1 container (15 ounces) part-skim ricotta cheese
2 eggs, beaten
¼ cup grated Parmesan cheese
1 box (16 ounces) ziti pasta, cooked and drained
1 jar (28 ounces) RAGÚ® Chunky Gardenstyle Pasta Sauce
1 cup shredded mozzarella cheese (about 4 ounces)

Preheat oven to 350°F. In large bowl, combine ricotta cheese, eggs and Parmesan cheese; set aside.

In another bowl, thoroughly combine pasta and Ragú® Chunky Gardenstyle Pasta Sauce.

In 13×9-inch baking dish, spoon ½ of the pasta mixture; evenly top with ricotta cheese mixture, then remaining pasta mixture. Sprinkle with mozzarella cheese. Bake 30 minutes or until heated through. Serve, if desired, with additional heated pasta sauce.

Makes 8 servings

Three Cheese Baked Ziti

Cannelloni with Tomato-Eggplant Sauce

Tomato-Eggplant Sauce
(recipe follows)
1 package (10 ounces) fresh
   spinach
1 cup fat-free ricotta cheese
4 egg whites, beaten
¼ cup (1 ounce) grated
   Parmesan cheese
2 tablespoons finely chopped
   fresh parsley
½ teaspoon salt (optional)
8 manicotti (about 4 ounces),
   cooked and cooled
1 cup (4 ounces) shredded
   reduced-fat mozzarella
   cheese

1. Preheat oven to 350°F. Prepare Tomato-Eggplant Sauce.

2. Wash spinach; do not pat dry. Place spinach in saucepan; cook, covered, over medium-high heat 3 to 5 minutes or until spinach is wilted. Cool slightly and drain; chop finely.

3. Combine ricotta cheese, spinach, egg whites, Parmesan cheese, parsley and salt, if desired, in large bowl; mix well. Spoon mixture into manicotti shells; arrange in 13×9-inch baking pan. Spoon Tomato-Eggplant Sauce over manicotti; sprinkle with mozzarella cheese.

4. Bake manicotti, uncovered, 25 to 30 minutes or until hot and bubbly. Garnish as desired.

*Makes 4 servings
(2 manicotti each)*

Tomato-Eggplant Sauce

Olive oil-flavored nonstick
   cooking spray
1 small eggplant, coarsely
   chopped
½ cup chopped onion
2 cloves garlic, minced
½ teaspoon dried tarragon
   leaves
¼ teaspoon dried thyme leaves
1 can (16 ounces) no-salt-
   added whole tomatoes,
   undrained and coarsely
   chopped
Salt
Black pepper

1. Spray large skillet with cooking spray; heat over medium heat until hot. Add eggplant, onion, garlic, tarragon and thyme; cook and stir about 5 minutes or until vegetables are tender.

2. Stir in tomatoes; bring to a boil. Reduce heat and simmer, uncovered, 3 to 4 minutes. Season to taste with salt and pepper.

Makes about 2½ cups

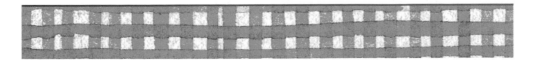

Cannelloni with Tomato-Eggplant Sauce

Wisconsin Swiss Linguine Tart

½ **cup butter, divided**
2 **garlic cloves, minced**
30 **thin French bread slices**
3 **tablespoons flour**
1 **teaspoon salt**
¼ **teaspoon white pepper**
  Dash nutmeg
2½ **cups milk**
¼ **cup grated Wisconsin
  Parmesan cheese**
2 **eggs, beaten**
2 **cups (8 ounces) shredded
  Wisconsin Baby Swiss
  cheese, divided**
8 **ounces fresh linguine,
  cooked, drained**
⅓ **cup green onion slices**
2 **tablespoons minced fresh
  basil** *or* **2 teaspoons dried
  basil, crushed**
2 **plum tomatoes**

Melt ¼ cup butter. Add garlic; cook 1 minute. Brush 10-inch pie plate with butter mixture; line bottom and sides with bread, allowing bread to come 1 inch over sides. Brush bread with remaining butter mixture. Bake at 350°F for 5 minutes or until lightly browned. Set aside.

Melt remaining butter in saucepan over low heat. Blend in flour and seasonings. Gradually add milk; cook, stirring constantly, until thickened. Remove from heat; add Parmesan cheese. Stir small amount of sauce into eggs; mix well. Stir in remaining sauce.

Toss 1¼ cups Swiss cheese with linguine, green onions and basil. Pour sauce over linguine mixture; mix well. Pour into crust. Cut each tomato lengthwise into eight slices; place on tart. Sprinkle with remaining ¾ cup Swiss cheese. Bake at 350°F for 25 minutes or until warm. Let stand 5 minutes.

Makes 8 servings

Favorite recipe from **Wisconsin Milk Marketing Board**

Tidbit

Pasta should be slightly undercooked when it is mixed with other ingredients in a casserole. It will continue to cook once it's in the oven.

Wisconsin Swiss Linguine Tart

Italian Eggplant Parmigiana

- 1 large eggplant, sliced ¼ inch thick
- 2 eggs, beaten
- ½ cup dry bread crumbs
- 1 can (14½ ounces) DEL MONTE® Italian Recipe Stewed Tomatoes
- 1 can (15 ounces) DEL MONTE® Tomato Sauce
- 2 cloves garlic, minced
- ½ teaspoon dried basil
- 6 ounces mozzarella cheese, sliced

1. Dip eggplant slices into eggs, then bread crumbs; arrange in single layer on baking sheet. Broil 4 inches from heat until brown and tender, about 5 minutes per side.

2. *Reduce oven temperature to 350°F.* Place eggplant in 13×9-inch baking dish.

3. Combine tomatoes, tomato sauce, garlic and basil; pour over eggplant and top with cheese.

4. Cover and bake at 350°F, 30 minutes or until heated through. Sprinkle with grated Parmesan cheese, if desired.
Makes 4 servings

Prep Time: 15 minutes
Cook Time: 30 minutes

Chili Relleno Casserole

- 1½ cups (6 ounces) SARGENTO® Light 4 Cheese Mexican Shredded Cheese or SARGENTO® Light Shredded Cheese for Tacos, divided
- 1 can (12 ounces) evaporated skim milk
- ¾ cup (6 ounces) fat-free liquid egg substitute or 3 eggs, beaten
- 6 (7-inch) corn tortillas, torn into 2-inch pieces
- 2 cans (4 ounces each) chopped green chilies
- ½ cup mild chunky salsa
- ¼ teaspoon salt (optional)
- 2 tablespoons chopped fresh cilantro
  Light or fat-free sour cream (optional)

1. Coat 10-inch deep dish pie plate or 8-inch square baking dish with nonstick cooking spray. In medium bowl, combine 1 cup cheese, milk, egg substitute, tortillas, chilies, salsa and salt, if desired. Mix well; pour into prepared dish.

2. Bake at 375°F 30 to 32 minutes or until set. Remove from oven; sprinkle with remaining ½ cup cheese and cilantro. Return to oven; bake 1 minute or until cheese is melted. Serve with sour cream, if desired.   *Makes 4 servings*

Classic Stuffed Shells

1 jar (26 to 28 ounces) RAGÚ®
  Old World Style® Pasta
  Sauce, divided
2 pounds part-skim ricotta
  cheese
2 cups part-skim shredded
  mozzarella cheese
  (about 8 ounces)
¼ cup grated Parmesan cheese
3 eggs
1 tablespoon finely chopped
  fresh parsley
⅛ teaspoon ground black pepper
1 box (12 ounces) jumbo shells
  pasta, cooked and drained

Preheat oven to 350°F. In
13×9-inch baking pan, evenly
spread 1 cup Ragú® Old World
Style Pasta Sauce; set aside.

In large bowl, combine cheeses,
eggs, parsley and black pepper.
Fill shells with cheese mixture,
then arrange in baking pan. Evenly
top with remaining sauce. Bake
45 minutes or until sauce is
bubbling.   *Makes 8 servings*

Recipe Tip: For a change of shape,
substitute cooked and drained
cannelloni or manicotti tubes for
the jumbo shells. Use a teaspoon
or pastry bag to fill the tubes from
end to end, being careful not to
overfill them.

Cannellini Parmesan Casserole

2 tablespoons olive oil
1 cup chopped onion
2 teaspoons minced garlic
1 teaspoon dried oregano
  leaves
¼ teaspoon black pepper
2 cans (14½ ounces each)
  onion- and garlic-flavored
  diced tomatoes, undrained
1 jar (14 ounces) roasted red
  peppers, drained and cut
  into ½-inch squares
2 cans (19 ounces each) white
  cannellini beans or Great
  Northern beans, rinsed
  and drained
1 teaspoon dried basil leaves
  or 2 tablespoons chopped
  fresh basil
¾ cup (3 ounces) grated
  Parmesan cheese

1. Heat oil in Dutch oven over
medium heat until hot. Add onion,
garlic, oregano and pepper; cook
and stir 5 minutes or until onion is
tender.

2. Increase heat to high. Add
tomatoes with juice and red
peppers; cover and bring to a boil.

3. Reduce heat to medium. Stir
in beans; cover and simmer
5 minutes, stirring occasionally.
Stir in basil and sprinkle with
cheese.   *Makes 6 servings*

Prep and Cook Time: 20 minutes

Eggplant Crêpes with Roasted Tomato Sauce

Roasted Tomato Sauce
(recipe follows)
2 eggplants (about 8 to 9 inches
long), cut lengthwise into
18 (¼-inch-thick) slices
Nonstick olive oil cooking
spray
1 package (10 ounces) frozen
chopped spinach, thawed
and pressed dry
1 cup ricotta cheese
½ cup grated Parmesan cheese
1¼ cups (5 ounces) shredded
Gruyère* cheese
Fresh oregano leaves for
garnish

*Gruyère cheese is a Swiss cheese that
has been aged for 10 to 12 months. Any
Swiss cheese may be substituted.

1. Preheat oven to 425°F. Prepare
Roasted Tomato Sauce.

2. Arrange eggplant on nonstick
baking sheets in single layer. Spray
both sides of eggplant slices with
cooking spray. Bake eggplant
10 minutes; turn and bake 5 to
10 minutes more or until tender.
Cool. *Reduce oven temperature to
350°F.*

3. Combine spinach, ricotta and
Parmesan cheese; mix well. Spray
12×8-inch baking pan with
cooking spray. Spread spinach
mixture evenly onto eggplant slices;
roll up slices, beginning at short
ends. Place rolls, seam sides
down, in baking dish.

4. Cover dish with foil. Bake
25 minutes. Uncover; sprinkle
rolls with Gruyère cheese. Bake,
uncovered, 5 minutes more or
until cheese is melted.

5. Serve with Roasted Tomato
Sauce. Garnish, if desired.
Makes 4 to 6 servings

Roasted Tomato Sauce

20 ripe plum tomatoes (about
2⅔ pounds), cut into
halves and seeded
3 tablespoons olive oil, divided
½ teaspoon salt
⅓ cup minced fresh basil
½ teaspoon black pepper

Toss tomatoes with 1 tablespoon
oil and salt. Place cut sides down
on nonstick baking sheet. Bake
20 to 25 minutes or until skins are
blistered. Cool. Process tomatoes,
remaining 2 tablespoons oil, basil
and pepper in food processor until
smooth.   *Makes about 1 cup*

Eggplant Crêpes with Roasted Tomato Sauce

Ravioli with Homemade Tomato Sauce

3 cloves garlic, peeled
½ cup fresh basil leaves
3 cups seeded, peeled
   tomatoes, cut into quarters
2 tablespoons tomato paste
2 tablespoons commercial fat-
   free Italian salad dressing
1 tablespoon balsamic vinegar
¼ teaspoon black pepper
1 package (9 ounces)
   refrigerated reduced-fat
   cheese ravioli
2 cups shredded spinach leaves
1 cup (4 ounces) shredded
   part-skim mozzarella
   cheese

MICROWAVE DIRECTIONS

1. To prepare tomato sauce, process garlic in food processor until coarsely chopped. Add basil; process until coarsely chopped. Add tomatoes, tomato paste, salad dressing, vinegar and pepper; process, using on/off pulsing action, until tomatoes are chopped.

2. Spray 9-inch square microwavable dish with nonstick cooking spray. Spread 1 cup tomato sauce in dish. Layer half of ravioli and spinach over tomato sauce. Repeat layers with 1 cup tomato sauce and remaining ravioli and spinach. Top with remaining 1 cup of tomato sauce.

3. Cover with plastic wrap; refrigerate 1 to 8 hours. Vent plastic wrap. Microwave at MEDIUM (50% power) 20 minutes or until pasta is tender and hot. Sprinkle with cheese. Microwave at HIGH 3 minutes or just until cheese melts. Let stand, covered, 5 minutes before serving. Garnish, if desired.   *Makes 6 servings*

Tidbit

Balsamic vinegar is an Italian aged vinegar with a distinctive mellow flavor. Its dark brown color is derived from the barrels in which it is aged. Look for it in the imported section of a supermarket or in a specialty food shop.

Ravioli with Homemade Tomato Sauce

Eggplant Squash Bake

½ cup chopped onion
 1 clove garlic, minced
   Nonstick olive oil cooking spray
 1 cup part-skim ricotta cheese
 1 jar (4 ounces) diced pimiento, drained
¼ cup grated Parmesan cheese
 2 tablespoons fat-free (skim) milk
1½ teaspoons dried marjoram
¾ teaspoon dried tarragon
¼ teaspoon ground nutmeg
¼ teaspoon salt
¼ teaspoon black pepper
 1 cup no-sugar-added meatless spaghetti sauce, divided
½ pound eggplant, peeled and cut into thin crosswise slices
 6 ounces zucchini, cut in half, then lengthwise into thin slices
 6 ounces yellow summer squash, cut in half, then lengthwise into thin slices
 2 tablespoons shredded part-skim mozzarella cheese

1. Combine onion and garlic in medium microwavable bowl. Spray lightly with cooking spray. Microwave at HIGH 1 minute.

2. Add ricotta, pimiento, Parmesan, milk, herbs and spices.

3. Spray 9- or 10-inch round microwavable baking dish with cooking spray. Spread ⅓ cup spaghetti sauce onto bottom of dish. Layer half of eggplant, zucchini and summer squash in dish; spoon on ricotta cheese mixture. Repeat layering with remaining eggplant, zucchini and summer squash. Top with remaining ⅔ cup spaghetti sauce.

4. Cover with vented plastic wrap. Microwave at HIGH 17 to 19 minutes or until vegetables are tender, rotating dish every 6 minutes. Top with mozzarella cheese. Let stand 10 minutes before serving.   *Makes 4 servings*

Tidbit

Eggplant comes in a variety of shapes, colors and sizes. Look for a firm eggplant that is heavy for its size. It should have a tight, glossy, deeply-colored skin. The stem should be bright green. Dull skin and rust-colored spots are signs of old age.

Eggplant Squash Bake

Dishy Sides

1-2-3 Cheddar Broccoli Casserole

1 jar (16 ounces) RAGÚ®
    Cheese Creations!® Double
    Cheddar Sauce
2 boxes (10 ounces each)
    frozen broccoli florets,
    thawed
¼ cup plain or Italian seasoned
    dry bread crumbs
1 tablespoon margarine or
    butter, melted

1. Preheat oven to 350°F. In 1½-quart casserole, combine Ragú Cheese Creations! Sauce and broccoli.

2. Evenly top with bread crumbs combined with margarine.

3. Bake uncovered 20 minutes or until bread crumbs are golden and broccoli is tender.

Makes 6 servings

Tip: Substitute your favorite frozen vegetables for broccoli florets.

Prep Time: 5 minutes
Cook Time: 20 minutes

pg. 232

pg. 238

1-2-3 Cheddar Broccoli Casserole

Roasted Red Pepper & Tomato Casserole

1 jar (12 ounces) roasted red peppers, drained
1½ teaspoons red wine vinegar
1 teaspoon olive oil
1 clove garlic, minced
¼ teaspoon salt
¼ teaspoon black pepper
⅓ cup grated Parmesan cheese, divided
3 medium tomatoes (about 1½ pounds), sliced
½ cup (about 1 ounce) herb-flavored croutons, crushed

1. Combine red peppers, vinegar, oil, garlic, salt and black pepper in food processor; process, using on/off pulsing action, 1 minute or until slightly chunky. Reserve 2 tablespoons cheese for garnish. Stir remaining cheese into red pepper mixture.

2. Arrange tomato slices in 8-inch round microwavable baking dish; microwave at HIGH 1 minute. Spoon red pepper mixture on top; microwave at HIGH 2 to 3 minutes or until tomatoes are slightly soft.

3. Sprinkle with reserved cheese and croutons. Garnish, if desired.

Makes 6 servings

Sweet Potato Crisp

1 can (40 ounces) cut sweet potatoes, drained
1 package (8 ounces) PHILADELPHIA® Cream Cheese, softened
¾ cup firmly packed brown sugar, divided
¼ teaspoon ground cinnamon
1 cup chopped apples
⅔ cup chopped cranberries
½ cup flour
½ cup old-fashioned or quick-cooking oats, uncooked
⅓ cup butter or margarine
¼ cup chopped pecans

MIX sweet potatoes, cream cheese, ¼ cup of the sugar and cinnamon with electric mixer on medium speed until well blended. Spoon into 1½-quart casserole or 10×6-inch baking dish. Top with apples and cranberries.

MIX flour, oats and remaining ½ cup sugar in medium bowl; cut in butter until mixture resembles coarse crumbs. Stir in pecans. Sprinkle over fruit.

BAKE at 350°F for 35 to 40 minutes or until thoroughly heated.

Makes 8 servings

Prep: 20 minutes
Bake: 40 minutes

Roasted Red Pepper & Tomato Casserole

Potatoes Au Gratin

4 to 6 medium unpeeled
  baking potatoes (about
  2 pounds)
2 cups (8 ounces) shredded
  Cheddar cheese
1 cup (4 ounces) shredded
  Swiss cheese
2 tablespoons butter or
  margarine
3 tablespoons all-purpose flour
2½ cups milk
2 tablespoons Dijon mustard
¼ teaspoon salt
¼ teaspoon black pepper

1. Preheat oven to 400°F. Grease
13×9-inch baking dish.

2. Cut potatoes into thin slices.
Layer potatoes in prepared dish.
Top with cheeses.

3. Melt butter in medium
saucepan over medium heat. Stir
in flour; cook 1 minute. Stir in
milk, mustard, salt and pepper;
bring to a boil. Reduce heat and
cook, stirring constantly, until
mixture thickens. Pour milk
mixture over cheese.

4. Cover pan with foil. Bake
30 minutes. Remove foil and bake
15 to 20 minutes more or until
potatoes are tender and top is
brown. Remove from oven and let
stand 10 minutes before serving.
Garnish, if desired.

Makes 6 to 8 servings

Zucchini al Forno

1 tablespoon olive oil
3 small zucchini (1 pound),
  thinly sliced
1 package (12 ounces)
  mushrooms, wiped clean
  and thinly sliced
1 jar (14 ounces) marinara
  sauce
1⅓ cups *French's*® *Taste
  Toppers*™ French Fried
  Onions, divided
½ cup ricotta cheese
⅓ cup grated Parmesan cheese
¼ cup milk
1 egg

Preheat oven to 375°F. Grease
2-quart oblong baking dish. Heat
oil in large nonstick skillet. Add
zucchini and mushrooms; cook
and stir about 3 minutes or until
crisp-tender. Stir in marinara sauce
and ⅔ cup **Taste Toppers**. Pour
into prepared baking dish.

Combine cheeses, milk and egg in
medium bowl; mix until well
blended. Spread cheese mixture
over vegetable mixture.

Bake, uncovered, 30 minutes or
until cheese layer is set. Sprinkle
with remaining ⅔ cup **Taste
Toppers**. Bake 3 minutes or until
Taste Toppers are golden.

Makes 4 to 6 servings

Prep Time: 15 minutes
Cook Time: 36 minutes

Potatoes Au Gratin

French's® Original Green Bean Casserole

1 can (10¾ ounces) condensed cream of mushroom soup
¾ cup milk
⅛ teaspoon pepper
2 packages (9 ounces each) frozen cut green beans, thawed*
1⅓ cups *French's*® *Taste Toppers*™ French Fried Onions, divided

*Substitute 2 cans (14½ ounces each) cut green beans, drained, for frozen green beans.

1. Preheat oven to 350°F. Combine soup, milk and pepper in 1½-quart casserole; stir until well blended. Stir in beans and ⅔ cup **Taste Toppers**.

2. Bake, uncovered, 30 minutes or until hot; stir. Sprinkle with remaining ⅔ cup **Taste Toppers**. Bake 5 minutes or until **Taste Toppers** are golden brown.

Makes 6 servings

Microwave Directions: Prepare green bean mixture as above; pour into 1½-quart microwave-safe casserole. Cover with vented plastic wrap. Microwave on HIGH 8 to 10 minutes or until heated through, stirring halfway. Uncover. Top with remaining **Taste Toppers**. Cook 1 minute until **Taste Toppers** are golden. Let stand 5 minutes.

Substitution: You may substitute 4 cups cooked, cut fresh green beans for the frozen or canned.

Prep Time: 5 minutes
Cook Time: 35 minutes

Creamy Mac & Cheese Alfredo

8 ounces elbow macaroni, cooked and drained
1 jar (16 ounces) RAGÚ® Cheese Creations!® Classic Alfredo Sauce
¾ cup chicken broth
¼ cup plain dry bread crumbs
2 tablespoons grated Parmesan cheese (optional)

1. Preheat oven to 350°F. In large bowl, combine hot macaroni, Ragú Cheese Creations! Sauce and broth. Season, if desired, with salt and pepper.

2. In 1-quart baking dish, spoon macaroni mixture; sprinkle with bread crumbs and cheese. Bake uncovered 25 minutes or until heated through.

Makes 4 servings

Prep Time: 10 minutes
Cook Time: 25 minutes

Autumn Casserole

¼ cup fat-free reduced-sodium chicken broth or water
2 cups sliced mushrooms
2 cups washed, stemmed and chopped fresh spinach
1 cup diced red bell pepper
1 clove garlic, minced
1 cup cooked spaghetti squash
¼ teaspoon salt
¼ teaspoon black pepper
⅛ teaspoon dried Italian seasoning
⅛ teaspoon red pepper flakes (optional)
¼ cup grated Parmesan cheese

1. Preheat oven to 350°F. Spray 1-quart casserole with nonstick cooking spray.

2. Heat chicken broth in medium saucepan. Add mushrooms, spinach, bell pepper and garlic. Cook 10 minutes or until vegetables are tender, stirring frequently. Stir in squash. Add salt, black pepper, Italian seasoning and red pepper flakes, if desired.

3. Spoon into prepared casserole. Sprinkle with cheese. Bake 5 to 10 minutes or until cheese melts.
Makes 6 (½-cup) servings

Lemon Rice Pilaf

1 onion, minced
¼ cup FLEISCHMANN'S® Original Margarine, divided
2 cups long-grain rice, uncooked
2 (14½-ounce) cans chicken broth
2 tablespoons lemon juice
2 teaspoons grated lemon peel
1 bay leaf
  Salt and freshly ground black pepper, to taste
2 tablespoons minced fresh parsley or 2 teaspoons dried parsley flakes
2 tablespoons pine nuts, toasted

1. Cook and stir onion in 3 tablespoons margarine in large saucepan over medium-high heat for 3 minutes. Add rice, stirring to coat well.

2. Add broth, lemon juice, lemon peel, bay leaf and salt and pepper to taste. Heat to a boil; reduce heat to low. Cover; cook for 15 to 20 minutes or until liquid is absorbed. Remove from heat; let stand 5 minutes.

3. Mix remaining 1 tablespoon margarine, parsley and pine nuts into rice. Serve immediately.
Makes 4 to 6 servings

Preparation Time: 10 minutes
Cook Time: 25 minutes
Total Time: 35 minutes

Apple-Rice Medley

1 package (6 ounces) long-
   grain and wild rice mix
1 cup (4 ounces) shredded
   mild Cheddar cheese,
   divided
1 cup chopped Washington
   Golden Delicious apple
1 cup sliced mushrooms
½ cup thinly sliced celery

Prepare rice mix according to package directions. Preheat oven to 350°F. Add ½ cup cheese, apple, mushrooms and celery to rice; toss to combine. Spoon mixture into 1-quart casserole dish. Bake 15 minutes. Top with remaining ½ cup cheese; bake until cheese melts, about 10 minutes.

MICROWAVE DIRECTIONS
Combine cooked rice, ½ cup cheese, apple, mushrooms and celery as directed; spoon mixture into 1-quart microwave-safe dish. Microwave at HIGH 3 to 4 minutes or until heated through. Top with remaining ½ cup cheese; microwave at HIGH 1 minute or until cheese melts.

Makes 4 servings

Favorite recipe from **Washington Apple Commission**

Crunchy Onion Stuffing

1 package (8 ounces)
   herb-seasoned stuffing
1⅓ cups *French's*® *Taste
   Toppers*™ French Fried
   Onions, divided
½ cup finely chopped celery
½ cup finely chopped carrots
1 can (14½ ounces) reduced-
   sodium chicken broth
1 egg, beaten

Combine stuffing, ⅔ *cup* **Taste Toppers** and vegetables in 2-quart microwavable shallow casserole. Mix broth and egg in small bowl; pour over stuffing. Stir to coat evenly. Cover; microwave on HIGH 10 minutes* or until vegetables are tender, stirring halfway through cooking time. Sprinkle with remaining ⅔ *cup* **Taste Toppers**. Microwave 1 minute or until **Taste Toppers** are golden. *Makes 6 servings*

*Or bake, covered, in preheated 350°F oven 40 to 45 minutes.

Tip: For a moister stuffing, add up to ½ cup water to chicken broth. You may add ½ cup cooked sausage or 2 tablespoons crumbled, cooked bacon to stuffing, if desired.

Prep Time: 10 minutes
Cook Time: 11 minutes

Apple-Rice Medley

Vegetable Parmesan Bake

1 envelope LIPTON® RECIPE SECRETS® Garlic Mushroom Soup Mix
¼ cup grated Parmesan cheese
1 large baking potato, cut into ¼-inch-thick slices
1 medium zucchini, diagonally cut into ¼-inch-thick slices
1 large tomato, cut into ¼-inch-thick slices
1 tablespoon margarine or butter, cut into small pieces

1. Preheat oven to 375°F. In small bowl, combine soup mix and Parmesan cheese; set aside.

2. In shallow 1-quart casserole sprayed with nonstick cooking spray, arrange potato slices, overlapping slightly. Sprinkle with ⅓ of the soup mixture. Top with zucchini slices, overlapping slightly. Sprinkle with ⅓ of the soup mixture. Top with tomato slices, overlapping slightly. Sprinkle with remaining soup mixture. Top with margarine.

3. Bake covered 40 minutes. Remove cover and bake an additional 10 minutes or until vegetables are tender.

Makes 4 servings

SPAM™ Corn Pudding

1 (12-ounce) can SPAM® Luncheon Meat, cubed
⅓ cup chopped green bell pepper
¼ cup chopped onion
2 tablespoons butter or margarine
6 eggs
2 cups milk
1 tablespoon all-purpose flour
2 teaspoons sugar
1 teaspoon salt
⅛ teaspoon black pepper
2 (10-ounce) packages frozen whole kernel corn, thawed and drained

Heat oven to 300°F. In large skillet, sauté SPAM®, bell pepper and onion in butter until tender. In large bowl, beat eggs. Stir in milk, flour, sugar, salt and black pepper. Add SPAM™ mixture and corn. Pour into greased 12×8-inch baking dish. Bake 1 hour and 10 minutes or until set.

Makes 8 servings

My Favorites

My Favorite Recipes

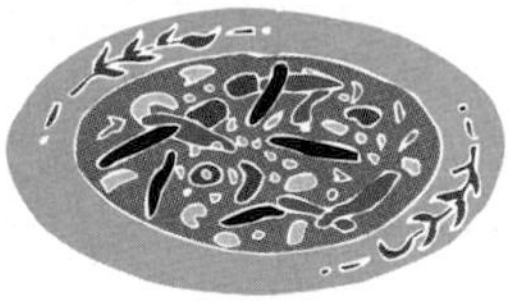

Favorite recipe: ____________________

Favorite recipe from: ____________________

Ingredients: ____________________

Method: ____________________

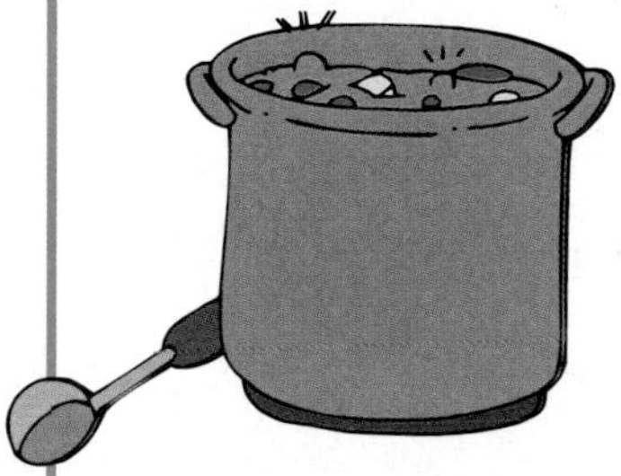

My Favorite Recipes

Favorite recipe: _____

Favorite recipe from: _____

Ingredients: _____

_____

_____

_____

_____

_____

Method: _____

_____

_____

_____

_____

_____

_____

_____

_____

_____

_____

Favorite recipe: _____

Favorite recipe from: _____

Ingredients: _____

_____

_____

_____

_____

_____

Method: _____

_____

_____

_____

_____

_____

_____

_____

_____

_____

_____

_____

Favorite recipe: _____

Favorite recipe from: _____

Ingredients: _____

_____

_____

_____

_____

_____

Method: _____

_____

_____

_____

_____

_____

_____

_____

_____

_____

_____

My Favorite Recipes

Favorite recipe: _____

Favorite recipe from: _____

Ingredients: _____

_____

_____

_____

_____

_____

Method: _____

_____

_____

_____

_____

_____

_____

_____

_____

_____

_____

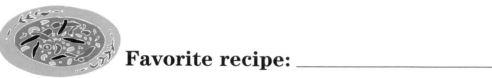

Favorite recipe: _____

Favorite recipe from: _____

Ingredients: _____

_____

_____

_____

_____

_____

Method: _____

_____

_____

_____

_____

_____

_____

_____

_____

_____

My Favorite Recipes

Favorite recipe: _____

Favorite recipe from: _____

Ingredients: _____

_____

_____

_____

_____

_____

Method: _____

_____

_____

_____

_____

_____

_____

_____

_____

_____

_____

Favorite recipe: _____

Favorite recipe from: _____

Ingredients: _____

_____

_____

_____

_____

_____

Method: _____

_____

_____

_____

_____

_____

_____

_____

_____

_____

_____

My Favorite Recipes

Favorite recipe: _____

Favorite recipe from: _____

Ingredients: _____

_____

_____

_____

_____

_____

Method: _____

_____

_____

_____

_____

_____

_____

_____

_____

_____

_____

My Favorite Recipes

Favorite recipe: _____

Favorite recipe from: _____

Ingredients: _____

_____

_____

_____

_____

_____

Method: _____

_____

_____

_____

_____

_____

_____

_____

_____

_____

_____

My Favorite Recipes

Favorite recipe: _____

Favorite recipe from: _____

Ingredients: _____

_____

_____

_____

_____

_____

Method: _____

_____

_____

_____

_____

_____

_____

_____

_____

_____

Favorite recipe: _____

Favorite recipe from: _____

Ingredients: _____

_____

_____

_____

_____

_____

Method: _____

_____

_____

_____

_____

_____

_____

_____

_____

_____

_____

My Favorite Recipes

Favorite recipe: _____

Favorite recipe from: _____

Ingredients: _____

_____

_____

_____

_____

_____

Method: _____

_____

_____

_____

_____

_____

_____

_____

_____

_____

_____

_____

Favorite recipe: _____

Favorite recipe from: _____

Ingredients: _____

_____

_____

_____

_____

Method: _____

_____

_____

_____

_____

_____

_____

_____

_____

_____

My Favorite Recipes

Favorite recipe: _____

Favorite recipe from: _____

Ingredients: _____

_____

_____

_____

_____

_____

Method: _____

_____

_____

_____

_____

_____

_____

_____

_____

_____

_____

_____

My Favorite Recipes

Favorite recipe: _____

Favorite recipe from: _____

Ingredients: _____

_____

_____

_____

_____

_____

Method: _____

_____

_____

_____

_____

_____

_____

_____

_____

_____

My Favorite Recipes

Favorite recipe: _____

Favorite recipe from: _____

Ingredients: _____

_____

_____

_____

_____

_____

Method: _____

_____

_____

_____

_____

_____

_____

_____

_____

_____

_____

_____

Favorite recipe: _____

Favorite recipe from: _____

Ingredients: _____

_____

_____

_____

_____

_____

Method: _____

_____

_____

_____

_____

_____

_____

_____

_____

_____

_____

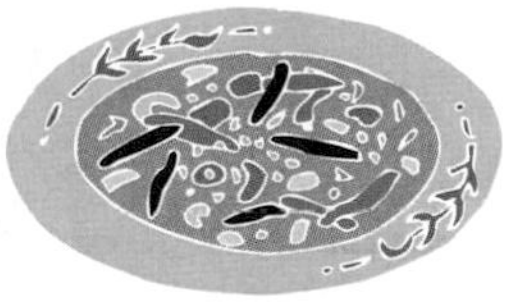

Favorite recipe: _____

Favorite recipe from: _____

Ingredients: _____

_____

_____

_____

_____

_____

Method: _____

_____

_____

_____

_____

_____

_____

_____

_____

_____

_____

_____

Favorite recipe: _____

Favorite recipe from: _____

Ingredients: _____

_____

_____

_____

_____

Method: _____

_____

_____

_____

_____

_____

_____

_____

_____

_____

_____

_____

My Favorite Dinner Party

Date: _____

Occasion: _____
_____

Guests: _____
_____
_____
_____
_____

Menu: _____
_____
_____
_____
_____
_____
_____
_____
_____
_____
_____
_____

My Favorite Dinner Party

Date: _____

Occasion: _____
_____

Guests: _____
_____
_____
_____
_____

Menu: _____
_____
_____
_____
_____
_____
_____
_____
_____
_____
_____

My Favorite Dinner Party

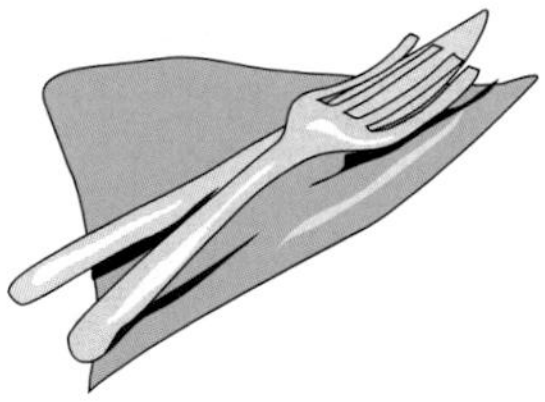

Date: ______________________________

Occasion: ______________________________

____

Guests: ______________________________

____

____

____

____

Menu: ______________________________

____

____

____

____

____

____

____

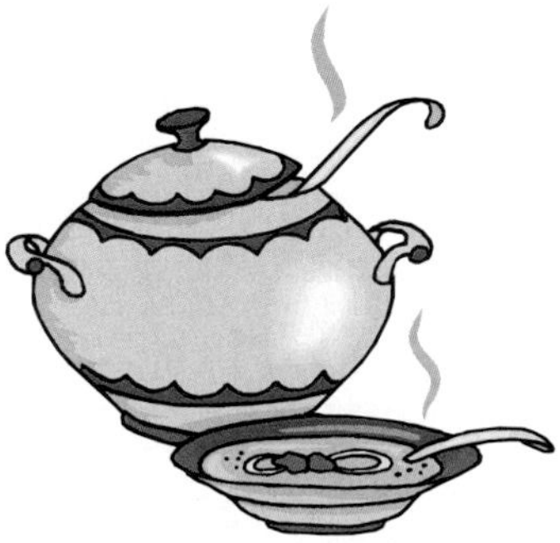

____

____

____

____

____

My Favorite Dinner Party

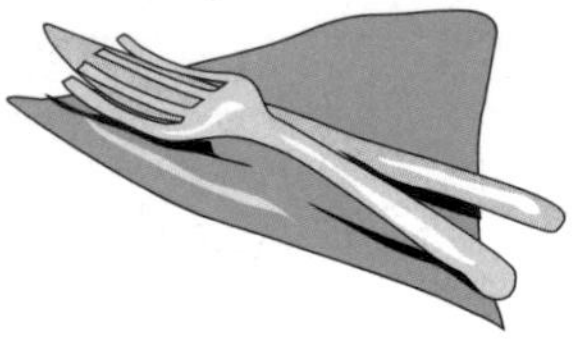

Date: _____

Occasion: _____

_____

Guests: _____

_____

_____

_____

_____

Menu: _____

_____

_____

_____

_____

_____

_____

_____

_____

_____

_____

_____

My Favorite Potluck

Date: _____

Occasion: _____

_____

Guests: _____

_____

_____

_____

_____

Menu: _____

_____

_____

_____

_____

_____

_____

_____

_____

_____

_____

_____

My Favorite Potluck

Date: _____

Occasion: _____

_____

Guests: _____

_____

_____

_____

_____

Menu: _____

_____

_____

_____

_____

_____

_____

_____

_____

_____

_____

My Favorite Potluck

Date: _____

Occasion: _____

_____

Guests: _____

_____

_____

_____

_____

Menu: _____

_____

_____

_____

_____

_____

_____

_____

_____

_____

_____

_____

My Favorite Potluck

Date: _____

Occasion: _____
_____

Guests: _____
_____
_____
_____
_____

Menu: _____
_____
_____
_____
_____
_____
_____
_____
_____
_____
_____
_____
_____

My Favorite Food Gifts

Friend: _____

Date: _____

Food gift: _____

_____

_____

_____

Friend: _____

Date: _____

Food gift: _____

_____

_____

_____

Friend: _____

Date: _____

Food gift: _____

_____

_____

_____

My Favorite Food Gifts

Friend: _____

Date: _____

Food gift: _____

_____

_____

_____

Friend: _____

Date: _____

Food gift: _____

_____

_____

_____

Friend: _____

Date: _____

Food gift: _____

_____

_____

_____

My Favorite Friends

Friend: _____

Favorite foods: _____

_____

Don't serve: _____

_____

_____

Friend: _____

Favorite foods: _____

_____

Don't serve: _____

_____

_____

Friend: _____

Favorite foods: _____

_____

Don't serve: _____

_____

_____

271

My Favorite Friends

Friend: _____

Favorite foods: _____

_____

Don't serve: _____

_____

_____

Friend: _____

Favorite foods: _____

_____

Don't serve: _____

_____

_____

Friend: _____

Favorite foods: _____

_____

Don't serve: _____

_____

_____

Hints, Tips
& Index

Casserole Tips

Casserole Cookware
Casserole cookware comes in a variety of shapes, sizes and materials that fall into two general descriptions. They can be either deep, round containers with handles and tight-fitting lids, or square and rectangular baking dishes. Casseroles are made out of glass, ceramic or metal. When making a casserole, it's important to bake it in the proper size dish so that the ingredients cook evenly in the time specified.

Size Unknown?
If the size of the casserole or baking dish isn't marked on the bottom of the dish, it can be measured to determine the size.

• Round and oval casseroles are measured by volume, not inches, and are always listed by quart capacity. Fill a measuring cup with water and pour it into an empty casserole. Repeat until the casserole is filled with water, keeping track of the amount of water added. The amount of water is equivalent to the size of the dish.

• Square and rectangular baking dishes are usually measured in inches. If the dimensions aren't marked on the bottom of a square or rectangular baking dish, use a ruler to measure on top from the inside of one edge to the inside of the opposite edge.

Helpful Preparation Techniques
Some of the recipes call for advance preparations, such as cooked chicken or pasta. In order to ensure success when preparing the recipes, here are several preparation tips and techniques.

• Tips for Cooking Pasta
For every pound of pasta, bring 4 to 6 quarts of water to a full, rolling boil. Gradually add pasta, allowing water to return to a boil. Stir frequently to prevent the pasta from sticking together.

Pasta is finished cooking when it is tender but still firm to the bite, or al dente. The pasta continues to cook when the casserole is placed in the oven, so it is important that the pasta be slightly undercooked. Otherwise, the more the pasta cooks, the softer it becomes and, eventually, it will fall apart.

Immediately drain pasta to prevent overcooking. For best results, combine pasta with other ingredients immediately after draining.

• Tips for Cooking Rice

The different types of rice require different amounts of water and cooking times. Follow the package instructions for the best results.

Measure the amount of water specified on the package and pour into a medium saucepan. Bring to a boil over medium-high heat. Slowly add rice and return to a boil. Reduce heat to low. Cover and simmer for the time specified on the package or until the rice is tender and most of the water has been absorbed.

To test the rice for doneness, bite into a grain or squeeze a grain between your thumb and index finger. The rice is done when it is tender and the center is not hard.

• Tips for Chopping and Storing Fresh Herbs

To chop fresh herbs, place them in a glass measuring cup. Snip the herbs into small pieces with kitchen scissors.

Wrap remaining fresh herbs in a slightly damp paper towel and place in an airtight plastic food storage bag. Store up to 5 days in the refrigerator.

Top it Off!

Buttery, golden brown bread crumbs are a popular choice when it comes to topping a casserole, but the selections shouldn't end there. Be creative with the many choices available to jazz up an old favorite or just vary how they are used. Crispy toppings can be crushed, partially crushed, broken into bite-size pieces or left whole. Fruits, vegetables and other toppings can be chopped, sliced or shredded. Sprinkle a new spice or herb in place of another one. All the toppings can be placed on top of the casserole in a variety of ways–a small amount in the center, around the edges as a border, or in straight or diagonal lines across the top.

Crispy toppings add a nice texture to your casseroles. Choose from crushed unsweetened cereals; potato, corn, tortilla or bagel chips; pretzels; flour or corn tortilla strips; plain or seasoned croutons; flavored crackers; crumbled bacon; ramen or chow mein noodles; sesame seeds; French fried onions and various nuts. As a general guide, add 1 tablespoon melted butter to ½ cup crushed crumbs, sprinkle over the casserole and bake.

Fruits, vegetables and other toppings add a burst of color to most casseroles. Add green, red or white onions; orange or lemon peel; mushrooms; dried or fresh fruits, such as apples, apricots, cranberries, dates, oranges, pineapple and raisins; olives; bell or chili peppers; bean sprouts; tomatoes; avocados; celery; corn; coconut; carrots; fresh herbs and shredded cheeses according to what flavor and look you desire. In order to keep the fruits and vegetables bright and crisp, add them 5 minutes before the casserole is finished cooking or sprinkle them on just after it's out of the oven.

• Homemade Bread Crumbs

Making your own bread crumbs is a great way to use up the rest of a fresh loaf. To make bread crumbs, preheat the oven to 300°F. Place a single layer of bread slices on a baking sheet and bake 5 to 8 minutes or until completely dry and lightly browned. Cool completely. Process in a food processor or crumble in a resealable

plastic food storage bag until very fine. For additional flavor, season with salt, pepper and a small amount of dried herbs, ground spices or grated cheese as desired. Generally, 1 slice of bread equals ⅓ cup bread crumbs.

The Basics

• As with conventional cooking recipes, slow cooker recipe time ranges are provided to account for variables such as temperature of ingredients before cooking, how full the slow cooker is and even altitude. Once you become familiar with your slow cooker you'll have a good idea which end of the time range to use.

• Manufacturers recommend that slow cookers should be one-half to three-quarters full for best results.

• Keep a lid on it! The slow cooker can take as long as twenty minutes to regain the heat lost when the cover is removed. If the recipe calls for stirring or checking the dish near the end of the cooking time, replace the lid as quickly as possible.

• To clean your slow cooker, follow the manufacturer's instructions. To make cleanup even easier, spray the slow cooker with nonstick cooking spray before adding the food.

• Always taste the finished dish before serving and adjust the seasonings to your preference. Consider adding a dash of any of the following: salt, pepper, seasoned salt, seasoned herb blends, lemon juice, soy sauce, Worcestershire sauce, flavored vinegar, freshly ground pepper or minced fresh herbs.

TIPS & TECHNIQUES

Adapting Recipes

If you'd like to adapt your own favorite recipe to cook in a slow cooker, you'll need to follow a few guidelines. First, try to find a similar recipe in this publication or your manufacturer's guide. Note the cooking times, amount of liquid, quantity and size of meat and vegetable pieces. Because the slow cooker captures moisture, you will want to reduce the amount of liquid, often by as much as half. Add dairy products toward the end of the cooking time so they do not curdle.

Selecting the Right Meat

A good tip to keep in mind while shopping is that you can, and in fact should, use tougher, inexpensive cuts of meat. Top-quality cuts, such as loin chops or filet mignon, fall apart during long cooking periods. Keep those for roasting, broiling or grilling and save money when you use your slow cooker. You will be amazed to find even the toughest cuts come out fork-tender and flavorful.

Reducing Fat

The slow cooker can help you make meals lower in fat because you won't be cooking in fat as you do when you stir-fry and sauté. And tougher cuts of meat have less fat than prime cuts.

If you do use fatty cuts, such as ribs, consider browning them first on top of the range to cook off excess fat.

Chicken skin tends to shrivel and curl in the slow cooker; therefore, most recipes call for skinless chicken. If you use skin-on pieces, brown them before adding them to the slow cooker.

You can easily remove most of the fat from accumulated juices, soups and canned broths. The simplest way is to refrigerate the liquid for several hours or overnight. The fat will congeal and float to the top for easy removal. If you plan to use the liquid right away, ladle it into a bowl or measuring cup. Let it stand about 5 minutes so the fat can rise to the surface. Skim with a large spoon. Or, you can lightly pull a clean paper towel over the surface, letting the grease be absorbed. To degrease canned broth, refrigerate the unopened can. Simply spoon the congealed fat off the surface after opening the can.

Cutting Your Vegetables

Vegetables often take longer to cook than meats. Cut vegetables into small, thin pieces and place them on the bottom or near the sides of the slow cooker. Pay careful attention to the recipe instructions in order to cut vegetables to the proper size.

Foil to the Rescue

To easily lift a dish or a meat loaf out of the slow cooker, make foil handles following these directions.

• Tear off three 18×3-inch strips of heavy-duty foil. Crisscross the strips so they resemble the spokes of a wheel. Place your dish or food in the center of the strips.

• Pull the foil strips up and place into the slow cooker. Leave them in while you cook so you can easily lift the item out again when ready.

Food Safety Tips

If you do any advance preparation, such as trimming meat or cutting vegetables, make sure you keep the food covered and refrigerated until you're ready to start cooking. Store uncooked meats and vegetables separately. If you are preparing meat, poultry or fish, remember to wash your cutting board, utensils and hands before touching other foods.

Once your dish is cooked, don't keep it in the slow cooker too long. Foods need to be kept cooler than 40°F or hotter than 140°F to avoid the growth of harmful bacteria. Remove food to a clean container and cover and refrigerate as soon as possible. Do not reheat leftovers in the slow cooker. Use a microwave oven, the range-top or the oven for reheating.

Weights and Measures

Dash = Less than ⅛ teaspoon

½ tablespoon = 1½ teaspoons

1 tablespoon = 3 teaspoons

⅛ cup = 2 tablespoons

¼ cup = 4 tablespoons

⅓ cup = 5 tablespoons plus 1 teaspoon

½ cup = 8 tablespoons

¾ cup = 12 tablespoons

1 cup = 16 tablespoons

½ pint = 1 cup or 8 fluid ounces

1 pint = 2 cups or 16 fluid ounces

1 quart = 4 cups or 2 pints or 32 fluid ounces

1 gallon = 16 cups or 4 quarts or 128 fluid ounces

1 pound = 16 ounces

How Much of This = That?

If you don't have:	Use:
1 cup buttermilk	1 tablespoon lemon juice or vinegar plus milk to equal 1 cup (stir; let stand 5 minutes)
1 tablespoon cornstarch	2 tablespoons all-purpose flour or 2 teaspoons arrowroot
1 cup beef or chicken broth	1 bouillon cube or 1 teaspoon granules mixed with 1 cup boiling water
1 small clove garlic	⅛ teaspoon garlic powder
1 tablespoon prepared mustard	1 teaspoon dry mustard
1 cup tomato sauce	½ cup tomato paste plus ½ cup cold water
1 teaspoon vinegar	2 teaspoons lemon juice
1 cup whole milk	1 cup skim milk plus 2 tablespoons melted butter
1 cup sour cream	1 cup plain yogurt

Is It Done Yet?

Use the following guides to test for doneness.

CASSEROLES
until hot and bubbly
until heated through
until cheese melts

MEAT

Beef
medium   140°F to 145°F
well done 160°F

Veal
medium   145°F to 150°F
well done 160°F

Lamb
medium   145°F
well done 160°F

Pork
well done 165°F to 170°F

POULTRY

Chicken
until temperature in thigh
    is 180°F (whole bird)
until chicken is no longer
    pink in center
until temperature in breast
    is 170°F

SEAFOOD

Fish
until fish begins to flake
    against the grain when
    tested with fork

Shrimp
until shrimp are pink and
    opaque

SAUCES
until (slightly) thickened

SOUPS
until heated through

STEWS
until meat is tender
until vegetables are tender

VEGETABLES
until crisp-tender
until tender
until browned

Metric Conversion Chart

VOLUME MEASUREMENTS (dry)

⅛ teaspoon = 0.5 mL
¼ teaspoon = 1 mL
½ teaspoon = 2 mL
¾ teaspoon = 4 mL
1 teaspoon = 5 mL
1 tablespoon = 15 mL
2 tablespoons = 30 mL
¼ cup = 60 mL
⅓ cup = 75 mL
½ cup = 125 mL
⅔ cup = 150 mL
¾ cup = 175 mL
1 cup = 250 mL
2 cups = 1 pint = 500 mL
3 cups = 750 mL
4 cups = 1 quart = 1 L

VOLUME MEASUREMENTS (fluid)

1 fluid ounce (2 tablespoons) = 30 mL
4 fluid ounces (½ cup) = 125 mL
8 fluid ounces (1 cup) = 250 mL
12 fluid ounces (1½ cups) = 375 mL
16 fluid ounces (2 cups) = 500 mL

WEIGHTS (mass)

½ ounce = 15 g
1 ounce = 30 g
3 ounces = 90 g
4 ounces = 120 g
8 ounces = 225 g
10 ounces = 285 g
12 ounces = 360 g
16 ounces = 1 pound = 450 g

DIMENSIONS

1/16 inch = 2 mm
⅛ inch = 3 mm
¼ inch = 6 mm
½ inch = 1.5 cm
¾ inch = 2 cm
1 inch = 2.5 cm

OVEN TEMPERATURES

250°F = 120°C
275°F = 140°C
300°F = 150°C
325°F = 160°C
350°F = 180°C
375°F = 190°C
400°F = 200°C
425°F = 220°C
450°F = 230°C

BAKING PAN SIZES

Utensil	Size in Inches/Quarts	Metric Volume	Size in Centimeters
Baking or Cake Pan (square or rectangular)	8×8×2	2 L	20×20×5
	9×9×2	2.5 L	23×23×5
	12×8×2	3 L	30×20×5
	13×9×2	3.5 L	33×23×5
Loaf Pan	8×4×3	1.5 L	20×10×7
	9×5×3	2 L	23×13×7
Round Layer Cake Pan	8×1½	1.2 L	20×4
	9×1½	1.5 L	23×4
Pie Plate	8×1¼	750 mL	20×3
	9×1¼	1 L	23×3
Baking Dish or Casserole	1 quart	1 L	—
	1½ quart	1.5 L	—
	2 quart	2 L	—

Acknowledgments

The publisher would like to thank the companies and organizations listed below for the use of their recipes and photographs in this publication.

A.1.® Steak Sauce

American Lamb Council

Bays English Muffin Corporation

BelGioioso® Cheese, Inc.

Bob Evans®

Butterball® Turkey Company

Del Monte Corporation

Dole Food Company, Inc.

Filippo Berio® Olive Oil

Fleischmann's® Original Spread

Florida Department of Agriculture and Consumer Services, Bureau of Seafood and Aquaculture

The Golden Grain Company

Hillshire Farm®

Hormel Foods, LLC

The HV Company

Kikkoman International Inc.

Kraft Foods Holdings

Lawry's® Foods, Inc.

McIlhenny Company (TABASCO® brand Pepper Sauce)

Mrs. Dash®

National Fisheries Institute

National Pork Producers Council

National Turkey Federation

Nestlé USA, Inc.

Newman's Own, Inc.

Perdue Farms Incorporated

The Procter & Gamble Company

Reckitt Benckiser

Sargento® Foods Inc.

The J.M. Smucker Company

The Sugar Association, Inc.

Unilever Bestfoods North America

USA Rice Federation

Veg-All®

Washington Apple Commission

Wisconsin Milk Marketing Board

Index

Index

Index